I DON'T KNOW WHERE I'M GOING—
BUT I SURE AIN'T LOST

By Jess Lair, Ph.D.

I DON'T KNOW WHERE I'M GOING—BUT I SURE AIN'T LOST

SEX: IF I DIDN'T LAUGH, I'D CRY

AIN'T I A WONDER . . . AND AIN'T YOU A WONDER TOO!

I AIN'T WELL—BUT I SURE AM BETTER

I AIN'T MUCH BABY—BUT I'M ALL I'VE GOT

By Jess Lair, Ph.D. and Jacqueline Carey Lair

HEY, GOD, WHAT SHOULD I DO NOW?

Jess Lair, Ph.D. in collaboration with Jacqueline Carey Lair

I DON'T KNOW WHERE I'M GOING— BUT I SURE AIN'T LOST

Doubleday & Company, Inc.
Garden City, New York

ISBN: 0-385-13392-8
Library of Congress Catalog Card Number 78–22795

*I dedicate this book to
my good friend Dave Petty
and to Baba Muktananda.*

CONTENTS

AUTHOR'S NOTE

The frightened little boy in me.

This is a very personal book, as personal as I can make it. So in one sense it seems superfluous to be writing to you apart from the book. But in another way there is a point to this.

If you were to ask me for the predominant feeling that runs through my life, I would say it is the frightened little boy. Only in the last few years has a good part of that feeling gone away. But there's still some of it there.

I find I can do things many of the people around me marvel at for the courage and the wisdom I show in those times. But even in times like those, there is a touch, or more, of the frightened little boy still there. So for me, I finally see myself coming to manhood in my fifties.

This note is so applicable to this book because the book talks of living a walk of faith. I can live that walk of faith a lot of the time. But it isn't all smooth and easy and natural yet by a long shot. I don't know whether it will ever be, or how much easier and more natural that walk of faith will be. But I believe in the walk. I'll trust my very life to it. And I'll wait patiently for any more smoothness and serenity in walking this walk that may be ahead for me.

But it is very important that as you read these pages you don't jump to the conclusion that these ideas I can talk of fairly easily are by any means second nature to me. They aren't—yet. So my best to you all.

Love,
Jess

I DON'T KNOW WHERE I'M GOING—
BUT I SURE AIN'T LOST

Chapter One

I WALK MOST SAFELY WHEN I DON'T KNOW WHERE I GO

This is a story that starts a long time ago, but most particularly it starts five years ago when, because of my books, I was invited to come to speak at Basel, Switzerland. In Frankfurt I met a Quaker who had brought Alcoholics Anonymous to Germany. He was not an alcoholic, but he saw the good AA was doing and brought it to Germany. His name was Heinze Kappes. I rode in a car with him from Frankfurt to Basel. While we were traveling, old Heinze Kappes said to me, "I walk most safely when I don't know where I go."

Four years ago I recognized the truth of that statement and realized it was something very, very important for me. And in the four years since then I've been trying to figure out what that meant; "I walk most safely when I don't know where I go."

Eighteen years ago I saw that my life was focused on the externals—what I could buy and what people thought I was. When I saw this, I committed myself to never again doing anything I didn't believe in. I soon found it was often very hard to know what I believed in and even harder to know what to do for me.

As I watched my life more closely, I came to see that there was an order and harmony in life I had never even suspected the existence of. I saw that trusting to the guidance in life worked out much better for me than my own fierce goal orientation. So now, finally, I was at a point where I was ready to turn my will and my life over to the care of God—as I understood him.

These books aren't written out of my imagination. They come out of my life. So what really happens when I see that I'm going to write a book in an area is that I need to have some experiences and some learning in that certain area—and I always get it.

This is so true that my wife, Jackie, often will say with some dread, "Not another book! Do we really want to learn about that?"

The learning and experience and understanding just seem to come. I don't go out looking for it. It just arrives in the area, and soon I am able to write down what happened and the reports are my books.

In 1977 I signed a book contract with Doubleday to write two books. One was *Sex: If I Didn't Laugh I'd Cry*, and the second was the book that was to be called, "I Walk Most Safely When I Don't Know Where I Go." When they got the contract in New York, the editors saw that there was no "ain't" in the title and they wanted an "ain't" to fit in with the other books I had written, which had that word in the title. So the editors came up with the title, *I Don't Know Where I'm Going—But I Sure Ain't Lost*. For the last couple of years I had been talking about writing the book *I Don't Know Where I'm Going* . . . but I couldn't get started writing.

One morning, my wife, Jackie, woke up and said, "Jess, you're going to write your book, and you're going to write it right now. But the problem is you can't write a book to their title, and that's where you got stuck."

I saw the truth of what she had to say, and realized I had something to say about the idea, "I Walk Most Safely When I Don't Know Where I Go."

Now, as it turned out, the book ended up with its New York title because it is a good title—but my working title was "I Walk Most Safely . . ."

Not too long after I signed the contract, about three years ago, I was sitting in a meeting and the other people weren't there yet, so I got out a book on the great religions of the world. I realized I knew a little something about all the religions except Hinduism. I realized I knew something about the Hebrew religion and about Buddhism and Islam, but I knew nothing about the Hindu religion, and I thought, "I'd like to learn something about that religion."

In those days I didn't know what saying something like that meant, but a short time thereafter some crazy little gal walked through my office door and proceeded to introduce me to two very crucial ideas of Eastern religion.

Now me with my Southern Baptist rigidity, I had enough trouble turning Catholic. I viewed Catholicism as a bunch of old Bohemian ladies with shawls over their heads praying to idols in some dark corner of a church! I told a priest this when I turned Catholic, and he laughed at me and told me that stuff was optional, but I still had trouble with my old beliefs. So the idea of an Eastern religion with a god with twenty-six arms and eighty-six legs and twenty-two heads was hard for me to swallow.

What happened is, this gal told me about a married couple and a man. She gave me a tape on marriage by a guy and his wife named Sharon and Jefferson Campbell from Polarity Institute of Orcas Island, Washington, which gave me some real interesting understandings of marriage. They had some ideas I already believed in, but the tape helped me to see far deeper into them. Their ideas came from their study of the Eastern religions of India and China.

Then the man this crazy little gal started talking about was her guru and teacher, Baba Muktananda. She said, "You've got to see Muktananda. You've just got to see him, that's all there is to it." And she literally grabbed me by the lapels and shook me.

What she said about him was that he was a person who is what they call, "God realized." A lot of people know about God. They know they are like God, they know that God is within them, and that God is love, but it's largely an intellectual knowledge. A "God realized" person is a person with a deep, overwhelming experience that floods the person and completely pervades them and wipes out everything else. It burns out all negativity. There's no more resentment, envy, bitterness, jealousy; none of the things that we think makes a person human. And this guy Muktananda was supposed to be a person like that. It was a pretty intriguing concept.

So, about a year and a half ago, I was in California and I stopped by Muktananda's ashram in Oakland. I checked in one night and the next day introduced myself to a woman there who knew I was coming and who knew I was a writer. She was a writer herself and became a follower of Muktanada.

The second day I was there she said, "Would you like to have an audience with Muktananda?" I said, "Yeah, that would be fabulous."

I had a chance to talk to him, and it was an unbelievable experience because I could see as I watched him that what they said about him was really true. He could meet these people from every walk of life and see them all just as pure love.

I heard a couple of stories about him while I was there. One was about a woman at the ashram in California the year previously. She had become a follower of his, and her mother was very angry that her daughter had become a follower. The mother came down to the ashram in Oakland to tell Muktananda how mad she was at him. She charged up to the door and they announced her. Muktananda ran across the courtyard with his arms open and said, "I'm so glad to see you." Her heart just melted at the love she was experiencing, and all the anger she was going to unload on him just went away.

The other story took place in the ashram in New York. A man came up to Muktananda in the receiving line they have to greet people. He stopped and said to Muktananda, "What would you do if I took out the gun I have in my pocket and shot you?" Muktananda said, "I would look at you the same way I am looking at you now."

Everyone there was so frightened, but Muktananda met him with love. It didn't necessarily melt the man, I don't know what happened to him, but it melted the hearts of everyone else there to see that kind of loving response from Muktananda.

When I talked to Muktananda they translated to him that I was a writer. His translator asked me the titles of my books, and she then translated them to Muktananda: *I Ain't Much Baby— But I'm All I've Got, Hey, God, What Should I Do Now? I Ain't Well—But I Sure Am Better, Ain't I a Wonder . . . And Ain't You a Wonder Too!* and the one I was working on at the time, *Sex: If I Didn't Laugh, I'd Cry.* Right away Muktananda smiled. He could see which way the wind blew, and he was intrigued. He started telling me things. One was about the power of sex, how sex is so powerful that one tiny speck of semen smaller than the head of a pin can create new life. He said that sex must be used very respectfully, always. Then I said something

about how those were some of t...
interrupted me and said strongly,
know what is in the book."

At the time I was a little taken aback...
that a book title has the essence of the b...
who is very, very wise can know everythin...
it was a very interesting thing for me.

He talked about some other things, and then... ...ow
long I was staying. I told him I was there for tw... ...y typical businessman's hurried trip. He said, "Here is a ...k on meditation. I want you to read this book twice. Then come back and
see me for eight days." Then he said, "You will learn the source
of all books." I said, "I will do that."

As I was with him I was having a very interesting experience.
I knew how important his time was. Ordinarily, about two to
five minutes is all the time anyone ever took. But I thought—
"I'm not going to leave this man's presence until I know it is
time." I wasn't going to excuse myself on the idea that he was so
busy I must leave. I knew I was going to sit there knowing that
it would be made clear to me when it was time to leave.

Finally, after fifteen minutes, the interpreter said, "We have
these other people to talk to, Jess, so will you please move back."
So I did. This couple came forward and he talked to them. Then
he looked around them and gave me this little jar of meditation
oil. Then he had two or three other things to say to me. I ended
up being with him for about an hour. It was such a great feeling
to me to be in the presence of such a great being and to feel his
love for me.

Now, I know he is interested in everybody, that he sees all
people as equal, but it was still a very lovely feeling for me. So I
said to myself, "I will read this book on meditation two times,
and then I will come back and see Muktananda." I knew there
would be an appropriate time to do that.

In the next year and a half I learned many things. I learned
that words are living things. What we think—is. I learned that
most everything we ask for is given to us in one way or another,
and I learned to be very careful about what I asked for, because
it usually came about.

Then Jackie went to Germany last February, and I wrote to

in Miami, Florida, where Muktananda was then, and
them I would come for eight days.

Jackie went to Germany under some unusual circumstances.
Her unusual circumstance was that she was going to try to decide whether she was going to come back to me. She was over
there deciding if living with me was really worth it or not. She
had a couple of alternatives, like divorce, or she could commit
suicide or run away, or some other equally pleasant things compared to living with me and all the hell she saw me dragging
along into her life.

On the outside I was saying to her, "That's all right," but inside my little Bricelyn, small-town-heart was quaking in its boot-
straps at the thought of being weighed and found wanting.

I went down to see Muktananda. His ashram in Miami was an
old converted beach-front hotel built perhaps fifty or more years
ago. It had deteriorated to the point where it wasn't an attractive property for hotel use anymore. It had been used as an old
people's home for a while and then been closed as a health haz-
ard. Muktananda's people came in, cleaned it up, and met all
the health standards. They rented it for a period of five or six
months for the winter so Muktananda could have his ashram
there. Then, in the spring, they would go back to the New York
ashram. Muktananda was spending a couple of years living in
different parts of America. He is a man in his seventies right
now.

In this ashram there are three or four people in a room. It was
very pleasant and the food was all vegetarian. You lined up with
a tray, like in the Army, and they put the food in the different
compartments. It was delicious.

It was so interesting. They had the garbage can right where
you brought your empty trays for the stuff that was thrown
away. Here were maybe four or five hundred eating, and the
garbage can had only an inch or so of waste in it after a meal.
Nobody threw anything away. They had that much respect for
the food—really for everything.

One of the things that you do in an ashram is when you are
walking down the hall, you don't make a lot of eye contact as we
do in this country. You don't come on with a big smile and hello.
You let each person be, and you don't make a lot of waves. You
don't disturb the place, and you be very respectful. You don't

smoke and drink, and at ten o'clock you go to bed. You get up at four in the morning and meditate from five until six. You have breakfast, and then you chant prayers for an hour and then you have a little rest and do some work and chant prayers before lunch. After lunch you take a rest and then in the afternoon you have a couple hours' work. My work was sweeping the court-yard. That's called "ashramseva," or work for the ashram. You learn a lot from this work that you do.

It was so fascinating because I didn't know anybody there except this one gal that I had met in Oakland, this writer, and she would talk to me briefly once in a while. So I spent the bulk of my time in silence. When I was talking it was to people I knew only casually.

It was so fascinating to watch myself in that environment. When I was doing my work or doing other things I would see the negativity that I had in me, yet there was nothing I had against anybody; nobody was doing anything to me. Still here I was being negative. I saw where my negativity came from. It didn't have anything to do with anybody around me, it was all coming out of me. It was such an amazing experience for me to see that so clearly.

Of course, that's what an ashram is. It is a clear, clear mirror to ourselves in which we see ourselves reflected. And like any mirror, the clearer the mirror the more accurately we can see ourselves as we truly are. The ashram was the clear mirror to me, and it gave the peace and the love that let me be quieted down enough to see and accept what I saw. So this is the thing that was so valuable to me there at that ashram. I saw myself so clearly.

As I was doing my work for the ashram I had some other very fascinating experiences. I would be sweeping the floor in my nice organized fashion and I would think, "Aren't I sweeping the floor a lot better than anybody else?" Or, I would be sweeping the floor and other people would be standing around talking, and I'd think, "Aren't I a hard worker? Won't Muktananda be proud of me when he sees me doing this, working so hard when these other people are goofing off?"

Each time I'd catch myself, "No dummy! That's not the point. You are simply working. You're not working for something or in comparison to something; you are simply working. You dummy!

You are just alive. And you are not alive in relation to something; you are simply alive."

In the eight days I was there I had about twenty-five hours of work for the ashram, "ashramseva" time. I don't think I had fifteen minutes in that twenty-five hours where I was actually just sweeping the floor. I was always sweeping the floor and thinking something. I would be going slow. "What if Muktananda sees you? You're going slow." Or I would be talking to somebody and think, "What if Muktananda sees you talking to somebody?" It was so fantastic just to see myself in that setting.

Then I had another experience that was so powerful. It occurred after four or five days there of meditating and living this smooth regularity. I saw that I really felt a tremendous feeling of love. Well, where did it come from? Nobody was loving me. I wasn't touching anybody, I wasn't holding anybody, there was nobody there I knew, so where was the love coming from? And then I experienced where love comes from.

Love is inside me! I discovered that the feeling that I had when I was holding somebody was simply the love I had inside me awakened or stimulated into existence. It was fanned into a flame strong enough so that I could feel it. So, what I realized I was feeling when I was holding somebody was my love awakened in me, just as they were feeling their love awakened in them.

Do you see what this means? Have you ever held someone and thought, "I don't feel anything. This person really doesn't care anything about me. I feel like I'm holding a stick"? That feeling is coming from us, not them. It isn't waking the fire of our own love in us.

I now see, through this experience, the terrible projecting we do in the name of love. Now I see there is no love in that. When we hold a baby we don't ask the baby to show us its love. No! We know it is our love awakened that we feel when we hold a baby. And we enjoy that feeling. It is a beautiful feeling. But with adults it's a different story. We hold them and mentally ask them to give us their love. If we don't feel anything, we blame them. We project our own difficulty into the other person! I had always felt that when I was holding somebody they were like a conduit and their love should flow into me. The burden that places on the people we hold and supposedly love is enormous when we have that attitude.

This was an overwhelming experience because I had been a person who had sought love constantly, feeling myself as being unloved, seeking love wherever I could get it, in any way that I could get it. Now here, all of a sudden I found I had been looking in the wrong place for love. "My God. I don't need to seek. I've got the gold mine within me. I don't need to do anything." And that was such a beautiful, beautiful experience for me.

I forget the circumstance that brought me to call Jackie in Germany, but I told her, "Hey! I've had a couple of real important experiences here. One is that the negativity that I'd blamed so much on you I see is in me. All those negative thoughts that I thought you had a hand in and were a part of, they're all here without you or anybody else having anything to do with them."

Then there was another thing. One problem I had suffered with in relationships with women was sexualizing those relationships. I would make a sexual deal out of a relationship with a woman. Not a "jump into bed with them," but there would always be a sexual overtone. Partly, I think I did this because sexualizing a relationship was a way to shut off intimacy, a way to react to somebody in a mechanical way rather than in a true intimacy where you react to a person just as they are.

For example, in Phoenix, where I was working out this book, there were my two friends John and Roland. They were two different people, and as guys, there was no question but what I was going to have two different relationships with them. They were each beautiful in their own way. Okay. With women I'm not prepared to have that kind of intimacy with them. I have enough trouble with guys, I have trouble with the whole world, but I have even more trouble with the gal half of it. I couldn't seem to react to women as separate people very well, so I would sexualize that relationship and act in a mechanical, stereotyped way with them.

Four years ago, I came to see the harm I was doing to myself by this fear I had of women. I saw that I needed to concentrate all of my sexual energy on Jackie as my wife. Then all other women would be just sisters to me. But I knew from long experience that old attitudes and habits die slowly, so I needed to be

reasonably patient with myself as I worked toward the new behavior that would come out of my new understanding and my
new attitude. I came to see that any sexualizing I was still doing
in relationships with women had to be kept out in the open for
my sake as well as the other person's. For our mutual protection.
That kept it from ending up in dark corners or in bed. So, at my
schools, where Jackie was working with me, she would see some
relationships between me and some of the gals at those schools
where there were sexual overtones. You know, the flirtatious bit
and the sexual messages, and this was very, very hard for her.

During the time I was going through this I could see that I
couldn't tell Jackie, "Hey, I'm going to stop doing that," because
I wasn't that far along. It would be like a new carpenter saying,
"I'm going to stop missing the nail and dimpling the wood." He
can't say he's going to stop that because he can't swing the hammer that well yet. Someday he's going to swing the hammer so
well that it won't happen but once in a thousand boards, which
is good enough to say it won't happen again.

Well, I couldn't say that, and it bothered me that I couldn't
say that. It wasn't that I didn't want to. I wanted desperately to
say that to Jackie, but I couldn't.

I had come to see that my sexualizing was coming out of a
couple of deep needs in me. One was seeking love. The other
was fear of closeness. When I saw at the ashram that love was in
me, I had a deep peace. I didn't need to seek love anymore. And
women could be people instead of people to fear while I sought
love from them.

This experience of love coming from inside of me was a very
powerful thing for me. For a long time I had the intellectual
knowledge that love was inside me. I told other people that. But
until I had the deep experience of love inside me, the talk didn't
mean anything. How could you describe the ocean to a frog in a
well? So, this experience of love made me see that my sexualizing problems were dead. They were as well and as safely behind
me as any old behavior can be. So, when I was talking to Jackie
on the phone in Germany, I was able to say also, "Hey, that sexual stuff that you've seen—it's all of a sudden gone. You aren't
going to see it anymore."

At that time that meant quite a bit to her. Later, the other thing, the not blaming her for the negativity that was in me, came to mean the most.

I had a final session with Muktananda; just a brief time. I thanked him for showing me the source of all books. The source of all books comes from meditation which puts you in touch with the very center of yourself. It is out of the deep part of yourself that all books come. The deeper I go into the true essence of myself, the more universal I become, and that is where the real books are, the true books, the best ones.

A few days later I was flying to Polarity Institute at Orcas Island, Washington, to work on their advertising, and Jackie agreed to fly from Germany to meet me in Seattle. But previously I had told Jefferson Campbell about some of the problems Jackie was having deciding whether she was going to come home to live with me or not, and Jefferson was under the impression part of the reason we were there was to work on our marriage. Often I don't make things as clear as I should, so although Jackie was surprised, we agreed to talk to Jefferson.

Right away he saw we had a couple of problems. One of them he saw was that I was not putting Jackie first. I was hanging on to Bozeman like it was a life preserver, and hanging on to friends and things in Bozeman and my routine. Jefferson saw that Jackie was dying from the lack of friends and stimulation of the type she needed in Bozeman.

He said, "Jess, do you want to put Jackie first?" I said, "Yeah." And he replied, "Then why don't you act like it?" I said, "Okay."

Another thing Jefferson saw was the problems we had in relation to our kids. They were all grown and not living with us, but there were dependencies between us that were hurting us all. When Jackie left and went to Germany she had said that it wasn't just me she was leaving, it was the kids too. She had often joked that if she ever filed for divorce she would name the kids as corespondents in the suit. So we were both ready to listen to Jefferson.

He suggested a six-month sabbatical from the kids. He allowed as how the kids would be as relieved as we would be to break this thing up. He wisely saw how all the traumas we'd lived through as a family had caused protective dependencies on all our parts. Our kids needed the vacation from us as badly as we needed a vacation from them. We all needed to see that we didn't need to live in each other's pockets.

Jefferson saw too that Jackie needed to be able to look at some alternative places to live. So he suggested that in this six-month sabbatical we go and live someplace else. He pointed out that what attracted me to Bozeman was that I loved beauty, so we should be on the look-out for a beautiful spot. He also saw that I needed the security of a small town so if Jackie wanted to go to Minneapolis, we should look for a small town nearby on a lake or with something else pretty to look at.

To do this we settled everything we could with the kids. We made what provisions had to be made with them in the beginning and told them there would be no contact with them for six months except in an emergency.

That was an eye-opening deal I'll tell you, because we'd spent thirty years in intense concentration with those kids. I had the worry that, if you pulled those kids out of our lives, there wasn't going to be anything left. Jackie and I had spent practically all of our time fighting about the kids, worried about the kids, pre-occupied about the kids. "Where's this kid? What's that kid doing?" We were afraid of what each kid was going to do, or wouldn't do. We would manipulate each other and try to control each other. It was a hell of a mess, I'll tell you.

Three of our kids had been through treatment for addiction the past year, and those relationships were especially hard, so we all needed this break desperately. Our other two children felt kind of tough about being included in the deal, but our deal with them hadn't been perfect either, so we felt we had to include them too. They all took it fairly well.

I thought Jefferson was right and that all of our kids would benefit from this plan. But I realized I couldn't get involved in whether they would benefit or not. I didn't intend this for a popularity contest. The benefit to our kids was their problem not mine. I couldn't worry about the results for them.

I found that I had mixed emotions about the deal, though. I had some deep attachments to the kids in some good ways and in some bad ways. But, as I'd said to Jefferson, if I was truly putting Jackie first, then there were some consequences and implications to that, and I'd better see it through.

In our time with Jefferson he had us write out what we

wanted and expected from what we were doing. He was pleased to see that our ideas about most everything coincided so well. In his view, they made sense to him too. He was pleased to see that we weren't as far apart as he had feared we'd be.

In the first month of this time three of our kids left Bozeman and Jackie said, "I think the pressure between you and me was more the kids than anything. Now I hate to leave this home in Bozeman I really love." But in Bozeman instead of spring rain we get snow, and so toward the middle of April we still had over a foot of snow in our front yard. Once again Jackie wasn't so sure that her much-loved home offset the Siberia outside in our front yard. So she prayed on the matter. Her bones ache in the prolonged snow we have, and so she was once again thinking, "I can't make it here."

To show you how strangely life works, we then had a powerful example of the deep mystery of life and how it proves out the title of this chapter: "I Walk Most Safely When I Don't Know Where I Go." Two years ago at our school in Bozeman, some people had come to attend from Phoenix, Arizona. Some of them returned to following schools. At our first winter School of Life in Bozeman a few months earlier there had been six people from Phoenix. Always they were saying . . . "You've got to come to Phoenix." This big, tall skinny guy said, "Fly in, I'll give you a car to use while you're there. Come to Phoenix."

We really loved these Phoenix people and we met some of them again at several conventions and always heard the same words: "You've got to come to Phoenix."

One morning in late April, the snow was still deep and Jackie was really asking her God for help. That afternoon the phone rang. She didn't know why, but as she answered the phone she said to herself, "Let this be an answer." It was. It was a woman from Phoenix calling to say, "Come to Phoenix." That settled that. Jackie told me that night that we were going to Phoenix.

I realized long ago that God regularly speaks to me through my wife, so we left for Phoenix with our travel trailer five days later.

That travel trailer is a funny thing, too. It is an expensive thing to have sitting by the side of your house, and after we hadn't used it for several years, Jackie said, "We should sell the trailer." I see now that God often speaks to Jackie through me, too, because I said, "No, we aren't going to sell the trailer. We might use it someday." Jackie thought that was a crazy idea. I wondered too why I had said no, but I did. So when the time came to go to Phoenix, Jackie and I took our little home with us, which was lovely because we both are so tired of hotels and motels and restaurants.

As we began our trip another funny thing from our past intruded. Several years ago some women from my old home town of Bricelyn, Minnesota, came to our summer School of Life. They stayed at the Holiday Inn in Bozeman. While they were there a Navajo Indian named Dave Petty came to sell turquoise in the lobby.

The morning after our school ended these women sat and talked to Dave all morning. They were taken by him, and Dave was taken by these lovely women. They got deep into philosophy and all sorts of things. A few days later I got a call from Minnesota from one of these women saying, "You've got to meet Dave." So I went and met him, and it turned out it was just like we were brothers.

Dave is about fifty-five years old and is a Navajo who never wants to see another hogan, so he lives in Lava Hot Springs, Idaho. He is still very much an Indian, but he is the only person of another race I have ever talked to where I was absolutely not conscious in any way about race. I thought Dave had always been the open, sweet human being that he is, but one day he told me a story.

In World War II he served in the Merchant Marine. His ship went down and he was lost at sea, swimming in the ocean. He said, "Jess, I went into that water a hostile, angry, militant Indian. When I was pulled from the sea, all of that was washed away." This explained to me what I saw in Dave. He had had a deep spiritual experience in that sea.

On the way out of Bozeman I told Jackie, "We're going to stop and see Dave. He lives right outside of Pocatello, right on our way." We got to Lava Hot Springs and found Dave. We had dinner with him, and he and I went in the hot thermal baths together and visited. But it was in the morning, when Dave had gotten the feel of Jackie, that he really began to talk.

Dave has some beliefs that are very different. They are very powerful beliefs, but listening to them is a little spooky. I don't understand them, I don't even believe them, but I respect them because I respect Dave so deeply. And there is always the chance that he is right. Who knows?

He has a thing he does with birthdates. He took Jackie's birthdate and said, "Jess, Jackie has lived many lives, she is a very old soul, and she is about ready to live her last life because her soul has moved through this process of many lives." As if that wasn't enough to hear, my wife looks at Dave and says, "I know. We always know about that last life. We know when the choice becomes ours."

"Now, Jess's soul is old but for a different reason," he continued. "He hasn't lived very many lives, but one of his lives he lived in the lost kingdom of Atlantis, and he lived for a thousand years in that one life. He was a very powerful, very wise man in Atlantis, but he fell into negative ways and lived for hundreds of years in egotism, self-centeredness, selfishness, pride, every negative emotion. He really lived that life, and he doesn't want any more of it, so in that sense his soul is very old too. And so, in this life he is dealing with ridding his soul of all of those things."

Dave doesn't care where the experts believe the lost kingdom of Atlantis was, he knows it was in the desert of Arizona. He has picked seashells from that desert, and he believes that the Indians living there are souls who lived in Atlantis. He believed that I was going home in a sense.

"When you come over the hill past Page, Arizona, and start down into the desert, Jess, look for the greeters. They are the women and children who have the roadside stands," Dave continued. "They are timid and shy so come at them gently, and listen to their spirits speak. Don't pay attention to how they're dressed or how they look. Just feel their presence. Really pay attention."

All the time I'm listening to Dave I feel like he's a guy explaining electricity to a kid in 1810. I not only am not understanding, I'm not believing anything he says. But one thing I do more and more is to make sure my attitude is open. Even though I don't understand or believe, I'm open. I put my disbelief aside, and if it works for me, I don't have to understand it. Even theoretical physicists don't understand electricity. But we all use it. We don't have to understand everything. If it works we use it.

Another thing Dave said in this conversation was that Jackie was my teacher and that I must listen to her. What an insane idea!

That idea reminds me of the story about a guy who served in North Africa during the war, and he met this Arab. He noticed wherever this Arab went, he was walking out in front and his wife was coming along behind leading the camel. Twenty years later this guy went back to North Africa to an army reunion and he ran into the same Arab. This time the wife was walking out in front and he was behind leading the camel. The old soldier wondered what was happening and wondered if women's lib had come to North Africa already. So he asked the Arab why the woman was walking ahead. The Arab replied, "There are still a lot of unexploded land mines left around from the war."

That story is a lot closer to my concept of women than the idea that Jackie's going to be my teacher! Intellectually, I think it's a lovely, lovely idea. Emotionally, I've got my heels dug in saying, "No way." It's like when two people marry for better or for worse, they really don't mean that "for worse" stuff. The minute it gets very bad, they split.

Jackie and I left Dave and started south. We both looked at each other in amazement. "Do you believe that stuff, Jac?" I asked. "I don't know, Jess. I just answered Dave with words that popped out of my mouth. I've thought about whether that stuff is true or not, but I've never answered yes or no to my questions. I guess I still don't know, but it sure makes life interesting to let your imagination go, doesn't it?" My wife smiled, and we drove south.

Twenty-four hours after talking to Dave, Jackie and I came over that hill just south of Page, Arizona, and there were no greeters there. We kept looking for them, but the roadside stands were empty!

I didn't know what this meant, but I kept my eyes open for alternatives. I've seen that things don't always present themselves just as we expect. So I kept my eyes open for other greeters, or greeters in other forms. As far as I could see there was just barren landscape. The only sign of life was a small store way down on the floor of the valley. It turned out the store was Bitter Springs. I suggested to Jackie that we stop and go in. The store was almost deserted. It was just a small post office and a place to buy necessities for the local Indians. It wasn't a tourist store, although there were a few rugs and some jewelry in an old case.

I walked around the store looking and listening as carefully as I could, paying attention to everything. It felt good being there, and I bought a Kachina doll of a white Buffalo Dancer. We talked a little to one lady behind the counter, but there didn't seem to be anything more there for us at the time. I felt peaceful and comfortable, but nothing more specific than that. So we left and began to drive through the desert.

Have you ever made that drive? If you haven't, you should. Even though I don't understand, there is something so deeply spiritual there. We stopped at one point and I got out and walked over to the edge of a canyon and looked over. The earth is different shades of red, and the landscape is awesome. As I looked over that edge I had the strange feeling that I had come too far. I knew that I was supposed to have stopped earlier to look. I don't know yet where I was to have stopped, but I will find that place someday. Even though I felt that I should have stopped sooner, I was suddenly aware that my bones were at peace. I had a feeling of the spirit of this place that made me think of how aware I was that Bozeman was "my spot." In a large sense, I knew that I had already been met by the spirit guides.

We arrived in Phoenix late that night, too late to find a spot for our travel trailer, and we spent the night in a parking lot, full of traffic noises that sounded like bombs going off to our tired brains. Both Jackie and I thought there was no way that this could be the right place for us, but we were willing to try it for a few days. We got settled in the travel trailer park and it was lovely.

We weren't there more than two or three days and I realized that the place was beautiful. But I had gotten my heels dug in because I didn't want to admit how nice it was. If I did, I'd have to stay. It was bad enough with Jackie loving it and wanting to stay, but if I liked it too, then I figured I was going to be there all the time and then all of my horses and friends in Bozeman were going to be taken away from me.

In a way I'm joking when I tell you this, but in another way I'm not. I hadn't been there very long when I realized that the mountains, the desert, the gorgeous trees and flowers made

Bozeman in the winter look like a dump. The warm air that caressed my little body, the foliage, the beautiful landscaping thrilled me. I saw Jackie riding her bike, swimming in the pool several times a day, getting a beautiful suntan. I saw her transformed from a pale dumpy housewife to a gorgeous doll in a few weeks. It took twenty years off her age in only a week or two! And my heart ached that she hadn't had this before when she could have had it. And my heart ached at the changes this suggested in my attached life. I had deep attachments in Bozeman. It was my spot, but in a way it was also my security blanket.

Jackie marched me at the point of a gun to the office and made me pay a year's rent. I did it with mixed feelings I'll tell you!

As we settled into our travel trailer and put an awning over our patio and got a shed large enough for me to use for an office, I began to pay close attention to this travel trailer resort we were in. I realized that we were in the perfect spot for us. We had been to many beautiful spots around Phoenix in the first weeks, but this place was our spot. I then realized that where we were living was like an Indian village. Here were all of these little tepees on wheels, living close together, just like a tribe of Indians.

And the makeup of those people! They themselves have no understanding of how unusual they are. But when you find a husband and wife who can live in a trailer eight feet by twenty feet long, all day together, month after month, you have got one very unusual husband and wife. And, furthermore, they have put themselves and their trailer in a community where they can't duck people. This resort is not like a trailer park. In trailer parks you can hole up in your trailer and never come out and no one will notice. But when you come into this resort you have made an unwritten commitment to be a part of that community life. Everyone is from someplace else and most of them are retired and they have no ties in Phoenix, so their deep commitment is to each other in this little resort of a thousand people. It's the same as when you were first married. Remember when we lived in the new suburbs filled with young marrieds? Our old single friends were gone from us, we were all in the same boat with a new life and new babies, and we were seeking new friendships. It's basically the same thing.

We found all kinds of ready-made friendships in Phoenix. We met people we felt we had always known. We were strangers, and they took us in. We went to parties and had friends to have fun with and play golf with. And there were groups we became a part of right away. So, when I could see I was ready to start this book, there was a group of people who wanted to hear what I had to say. For two long evenings I sat down with them and talked out the ideas that are in this book. Those talks are on a set of tapes.[1] While those tapes are just the rough beginning of this book, they are what it was based on. So here was another thing Phoenix and our spirit guides gave us.

Here's where I'd come from four years ago when Heinze Kappes first said to me, "I walk most safely when I don't know where I go." Then it was an idea I saw the wisdom of. I made the idea mine, but it was a head trip. At first I could intellectually say "yes" to this idea. But the past four years I had gone from the intellectual appreciation of "I walk most safely when I don't know where I go," to this recent set of dramatic experiences of truly walking most safely when I don't know where I go.

Doctors figure people can't change much past forty. Their attitude, by and large, is to just give them some pills and quiet them down. Don't take risks. I watched my wife, Jackie, take an ultimate risk. She stopped taking prescription drugs like tranquilizers and anti-depressants after twenty-four years of use and changed from a fat, dying woman of forty-eight to a young woman of fifty cavorting in a swimming pool in her new swimming suit.

You walk most safely when you don't know where you go because then you're so fully conscious that you don't know where you're going that you pay such careful attention to all the clues and signs. You walk in a meditative way, conscious of the present moment, and so you're safe.

It is when you feel that you do know where you are going that you get into trouble so many times. The reason for this is

[1] Set of 7 tapes—$35. Jesse Lair Tapes, P. O. Box 249, Bozeman, MT 59715.

that often when you think that you really know where you are going and why, you are just following your ego. The ego often makes us think we know when we don't know, and that is really trouble.

I have come to see that there are three aspects to my life. When I know I don't know where I'm going, I'm safe. When I think I know where I'm going that's trouble. When I'm sure I know where I'm going, that's disaster, because that is when I'm doing it all myself. That's when I really screw up. I have come to see also that of those three modes of life, I want to spend as much of my time as I possibly can not knowing where I'm going. That is really hard for me, and the rest of this book will be telling you about the methods I'm using and the problems I'm facing as I'm trying to get rid of all of the attachments, all of the opinions, all the excess baggage in my life, all of the things I think are so—but ain't.

It is like the story of the philosopher who came to the Zen master and said, "I would like to learn about Zen." The Zen master asked the philosopher to come to his home for tea. As the Zen master poured the tea into the philosopher's cup he filled it to the top and kept pouring. Soon the tea overflowed the cup and saucer and flowed out upon the table. "Stop, stop, the cup is overfull," said the philosopher. The Zen master replied, "This cup, like your mind is overfull with ideas and speculations. Until you empty it, there is no room for Zen."

This book is about how you and I can empty our cups and get rid of all that our mind is overfull of so we can make room for a new understanding—the understanding that only by surrendering our life each day can the Higher Power pick us up and put us in the spot that's just right for us.

Chapter Two

MEDITATION—HOLDING HANDS WITH GOD

Five of the most important teachers of my life were constantly stressing the importance of meditation. That's been going on for fourteen years. Yet I still don't meditate as regularly and as long as I know would be best for me.

The growth group I'm a part of says to meditate. An old friend kept telling me he would rather miss breakfast than miss his meditation, where he just sat and let his mind go blank. The Zen I studied kept saying there is only one thing to do, sit in meditation. Wally Minto of Alpha Awareness told me the one thing I should do every day is go within. And then Muktananda kept saying to all his people and to me, meditate, meditate, meditate.

Why don't I do the one thing I know is at the centerpoint, the one thing that will lead me closer to the God I seek? I see that my mind resists meditation. I now see that the only way I can overcome my mind is through a process of development. Over the years I have slowly and gradually built more and more of the things into my life that I know work for me, regularity in my life, going to meetings of my growth group, rest, relaxation, and a more unhurried way.

But it seems there is some kind of balance that must exist between my understanding and practice. It would be simple if each time I heard or saw a good thing, I would immediately reach out and grasp it in its fullness. But it doesn't work that way for me. I need to go through a gradual learning process where I come to understand and appreciate something and then gradually build it into my life. I'm happy with that. I've come to see that it is the right pace and timing for me. All I need to do is pay attention and be as aware as I can so I don't go too fast or too slow.

Meditation is already a tremendously powerful force in my life even though I'd guess I'm meditating only an average of two out of three days.

What meditation does for me, I see very clearly. The days in which I meditate, the scattered parts of me are collected, and they're all there together. Some of those scattered parts of me that are collected together turn out to be very crucial to me in handling some of the circumstances of the day.

It's just like a carpenter who has a full set of tools. If he's got a full set of tools, there's no job he can't handle. But if some of his tools are at home, some of them are at another job, and some of them are lost, about half the jobs he comes to he can't do right or can't do at all because he hasn't got the tools with which to do the job.

Now, by meditation, I mean something very different from what I used to think of as meditation. I mean meditation where I sit with my eyes closed, being completely quiet, keeping my mind quiet, and not trying to think about something. In a sense, it's a blank-mind meditation. I just sit down for a half hour to an hour in the morning and just be completely still. I get as close to an absolute blackness as I can get.

When I have a day with meditation in it, I get a lot more done in that day. I'm not scattered. When I'm too busy to take the time to meditate, I'm scattered and I don't get as much done. It's as though a bunch of people are shooting arrows at me and most all of them are landing, and it hurts. It's really troubling to me. When I have meditation, people aren't shooting at me. Occasionally I do see something coming my way, and I can duck or absorb it with no problem. When I meditate it's very seldom that I see myself going crazy in that day, even in a small way.

As I said earlier, Jefferson Campbell at Polarity Institute stressed meditation to me. Wally Minto of Alpha Awareness told me I should never let a day go by without "going within," which is what he calls meditation. But neither of their ways of talking about meditation were decisive for me. Muktananda's was. After I spent eight days at Muktananda's ashram and spent that time meditating each day for an hour and saw what happened to me, I saw that meditating would be a part of my life.

I had tried TM and Alpha Awareness, but like anything that we just dabble with we're dilettantes and soon we drop it. Years ago I had heard my old teacher say, "I'd rather miss breakfast than miss my meditation." But I didn't know what he was talking about. In all of the twelve-step groups, like Alcoholics Anonymous or Emotions Anonymous or Gamblers Anonymous, the eleventh step says, "Sought through prayer and meditation . . ." but I didn't know what that meant.

As I look around, I'm amazed at how little you see and hear about the value of meditation outside of the Eastern tradition. I see some references to it in the Bible like "go into your inner room . . ." I gather from some of my reading that a lot of the early Christian mystics and saints did it. Thomas Merton talks about centering, which is the same as "going within." The Quakers seem to use the word "centering" in this same way.

Someone once asked Catherine of Sienna why we don't feel God is a familiar friend. She said that the reason is because we've gotten away from the relationship of God being God and us being disciples. Instead we've gotten into the idea that we are the god and God is the disciple and his job is to do what we want him to do. It's like someone else once said, "We've made God a spiritual bell-hop."

We are incessantly chattering at God. We are always reminding him to take care of his world. We remind him of the starving Armenians, we remind him to have the sun come up in the morning, and so on and on. That's not a very effective way of talking to God as you understand him.

Meditation is the exact opposite of that. Meditation isn't just saying to God, "You decide what needs to be done and then tell me." It is even more opposite than that. Meditation is just being together with God in a quiet way for an hour each day—just holding hands with God.

Meditation is letting go. Once upon a time, a man fell over a cliff. As he was falling he reached out and grabbed at a branch of a tree sticking out of the side of the cliff. As he hung there and his arm was getting numb, he shouted, "God, if you're up there, please help me." Soon a voice up there said, "This is God. Follow my instructions very carefully. Number one, let go of the tree." And the man shouted back, "Is there anybody else up there?"

What God saw and the man couldn't see was that just a few inches below the man's dangling feet was a wide, safe ledge.

In searching Western writings for knowledge of meditation as viewed by basically Christian writers, I found very little on meditation as I understand it. It seemed to me there was a general confusion blending prayer and meditation. Meditation is a form of prayer, but prayer is not meditation. We often use the word meditation interchangeably with the words think, or ponder or pray. We say, "I meditated on the Bible this morning." What we mean is we read and thought about what we read and maybe prayed about what we read. This is not meditation in the sense I am using it.

You all know the experience of reading something holy and then sitting down and concentrating attention on that holy thing, thinking as hard as possible on the holy thing. Then we get up feeling very holy because we have done that holy thing and deserve a gold star. Then we go around all day waiting for someone to paste that gold star on us. This is what is so often thought of as meditation.

You can all see the problem. It's first of all fruitless for me to believe that I can attain by being a certain way. But even worse is the fundamental fallacy of my believing that anything needs to be attained. There's nothing to be attained. It's all done. This type of exercise (being concerned with attainment) is all in my mind. The mind sees everything as black or white, right or wrong, up or down. Reading, thinking, pondering, even most prayer, is of the mind. To me, meditation is of the soul, where no words are needed or even wanted. Meditation is silence.

Another fallacy I fell into was believing meditation was where I was silent, sitting there waiting for my marching orders from God. I thought it was holy to sit and wait for God to speak to me and tell me what to do. I see now that there isn't that much to be done. When there is something that needs to be done, like mow the lawn, God doesn't usually need to tell me about it. That's my ego. And like all ego things, when the ego doesn't get its marching orders the way it expects, it quits. It says, "this way doesn't work." Of course it doesn't work. It's not meditation. Meditation is meeting the God we pray to. I don't care if your

God is the Hebrew God, the Christian God, the Hindu God, the "old Indian," or any of the thousand definitions of God. Meditation is a going within to quietly hold hands with the God of your understanding. Meditation is going within yourself for the direct experience of God where you don't talk to him and he doesn't talk to you any more than necessary. It is like sitting and holding hands with somebody that you love. There is usually no need for words, it's just love. The God you pray to will be experienced.

When I first went to Transcendental Meditation, I was leery. I was given a Sanskrit word to say for a mantra to use in meditation, and there was a little ceremony using incense and foreign words. It was explained to me that repeating this Sanskrit word or "mantra" as they call it would take me within to a quiet place. There was no talk about God as such, but I knew this was a spiritual thing I was doing. TM emphasized that meditation was for relaxing and relieving stress, but I was a little worried that it wasn't Christian.

Now I see that my reservations were foolish. It is really stupid for us to believe that somebody else's God would come to us. There's no faith in that. When I meditate, why would the Hindu's conception of Kali with all of her arms and legs and things come to me? If I believed that would happen, I'm not showing very much trust or belief in my God.

In a way, I would have to say that meditation is the form of prayer for desperate men because only desperate men have deep enough faith to let go of the limb and drop, trusting that God has something better down below—like a ledge.

Most of you saw the movie *Butch Cassidy and the Sundance Kid.* A scene I'll never forget is when Butch and Sundance were being chased by the posse and they are finally driven to the edge of a high cliff. Far below is a river, between them and the river is a lot of space and jutting rock. They look behind them and see the posse riding up fast with blood in their eyes and their guns drawn. Butch and Sundance don't stop and confer. They just look at each other, let out a whoop and jump. They trusted that what lay ahead would be better than what was behind, and they didn't stop to debate.

We all jump off the cliff when our fear of what is behind us is greater than our fear of what's ahead. But the trust it takes to jump off! It took something very frightening to make Butch and Sundance desperate enough to jump, to trust in God. But once they jumped and were caught in God's loving hand, they weren't ever the same again. The second time they had to jump it still wasn't easy, but it was easier than that first time. And each subsequent jump got easier.

The most crucial issue in our relationship to God is trust, and in meditation as I see it, this lack of trust shows itself most clearly. In meditation we give up control. To me so many people who try meditation or write of meditation lack some trust. They are all saying, just as I did at first, "I want to control this situation so that some Eastern god or weird thoughts don't come out of the attic or the cellar, because then if that happens I'm in heresy, going against the rules of my elders or my past." And there we are stuck with our finite minds yelling . . . "Is anybody else up there?"

Life is always about letting go of that tree or jumping off that cliff. It's about trust. Until we have that trust nothing much can happen in our lives of a very spiritual nature. All fastening to religious form is lack of trust, a need to keep control with our finite minds. It is fear. Where there is fear there is no trust.

I am not against prayer. We need to talk to God. Prayer is beautiful, and I pray a lot. I'm not against churches or organized religions. We need them. They are our way of having some discipline, someone to answer to here on earth. Everyone needs that. I am saying that meditation has nothing in it that should dismay us or make us fear that we are going against our God or our religion.

Meditation is letting go with complete trust that our God will catch us and deposit us in a safe place. People who cannot do this have a small god, a limited god, and they must face this in themselves. I see many so-called Christians who have a devil who is much larger than their God.

Other than Thomas Merton, of our time, or Brother Lawrence of centuries ago, the Russian mystic who had the "Jesus prayer" and some of the old mystics, I have not been able to find many Christians who seemed to me to show this trust in their writings about meditation.

Where I am at this moment and at this time is to say that the only understanding of God is that God is complete love. And there is no mystery in God. Anytime we see a mystery or difficulty in understanding God it is our finite mind creating the problem. We are the mystery to ourselves because of our lack of faith, of trust, of understanding.

C. S. Lewis talks in his book *Screwtape Letters* about the character who dies and goes to heaven and sees all the experiences in his life that he thought were so awful fit into the tapestry of life like a piece of silk. There were no rough spots in the tapestry, it was all smooth. It all fitted together. But our rational minds can't understand spiritual things while they are happening. It's only when we look back that we can see how some awful things turned out to be very good.

I'm a teacher. I need to offer people hard problems to put them in experiences where they cannot escape except by thinking in a new way. That's what a Zen koan does. It breaks the bubble of rational thought. The koan, "Tell me the sound of one hand clapping," cannot be solved by the rational mind. The crucifixion of Christ can't be solved by the rational mind.

The koan and the cross make us see the limits of our rational mind and show us that we need to go beyond the limited power of our intellects.

Thank God if you are a desperate person, if you have immense pain. There is a great good in that. Only a desperate person is forced to trust, to have faith. Muktananda left home at fourteen and wandered the earth searching. He searched for thirty years before he found God-realization. Buddha left his life as a prince and walked away from a wife and a child and a kingdom to search for truth. That's desperation, and hand in hand with that there was trust.

In meditation I'm just a beginner. In the Hindu and the Buddhist traditions there is experience and knowledge of meditation that goes back for thousands of years. In the Christian tradition there were the old saints and the common people like Brother Lawrence who showed by their lives and their writing the power of meditation for them. But I don't see around me in current writing or practice much about completely surrendered meditation.

A long time ago I made a decision to turn my will and my life over to the care of God as I understood him. In my daily life I don't live up to that idea. I switch back and forth from living surrender to seeing myself take control. But I haven't changed my decision on prayer and meditation. Specifically, I made a decision to seek through prayer and meditation to improve my *conscious contact* with God as I understood him, praying *only* for knowledge of God's will for me and the power to carry that out. That "praying only" puts the emphasis on getting knowledge of God's will for me. I have come to see that the emphasis on "only" what God wants can come primarily in surrendering in meditation completely. I'm concentrating on that now.

It took my despair and all the desperate years to come into gratitude. Gratitude is seeing that God is in charge and handling everything that happens and that it is all good. Opposed to that attitude of gratitude is the attitude that we have to be careful of where we're stepping all the time because life is full of land mines.

In Africa in World War II, General Patton came up front to check on his units in that campaign to see why they weren't advancing. A couple of times he found that the reason they weren't advancing was because they were afraid of the land mines and were sitting waiting for the engineers to come and sweep the mine fields so they could advance. And Patton would say to his men, "Hell, there aren't that many land mines . . ." and he'd drive right through the mine field with his jeep. When he got to the other side he'd say, "Okay, follow this path. Come on, let's go." To me that attitude toward life is so powerful. The reason Patton could do that was not because he was a fool, but because he believed tremendously in his own destiny, and in a God who would lead him to that destiny.

We must believe in the God within ourselves 100 percent. We can't believe just 99 percent. With anything less than 100 percent belief there is always that little element of fear and doubt that contaminates everything and makes us defensive. When we are defensive we react with fear or anger. If someone says to me, "Jess, you're a lousy writer," I don't get defensive, so I know I'm believing 100 percent. But if someone says to me, "Jess, you're a lousy husband," or "you're a lousy father," I feel terrible because I'm not 100 percent sure of my ground in those areas. I know someday I will be because it is in my nature to be a husband and father. But for right now I'm not 100 percent sure of myself.

In other areas of my life I'm beginning to see that there are some things I am trying to be or do that I will never have 100 percent belief in myself about, because these things are not my basic nature. These things will slowly fade out of my life.

It's through meditation that we're able to get in touch with our inner self and to finally realize who we are and that we are 100 percent. And it is through this realization that we can become gentler, kinder, sweeter people. At the same time we become able to use our God-given power more effectively. Now I know most of us see a dichotomy between using our full power and being just plain, gentle, and sweet. But the funny thing is, the more we know we're somebody, the more we're able to be nobody special.

My wife had a poem from her childhood that she used to say.

> I'm nobody. Who are you?
> Are you nobody too?
> Good! There's a pair of us.
> Don't tell. They'd banish us you know.

You have to be somebody before you can afford to be nobody special. When you've gone the correct route, that poem is all right. If you believe you're nobody, that poem could be depressing. (It's by Emily Dickinson.)

In Thomas Merton's book, *The Way of Chuang Tzu,* he writes the following about "The Man of Tao."

> The man in whom Tao acts without impediment harms no other being by his actions, yet he does not know himself to be "kind," to be "gentle." The man in whom Tao acts without impediment does not bother with his own interests and does not despise others who do. He does not struggle to make money and does not make a virtue of poverty. He goes his way without relying on others and does not pride himself on walking alone. While he does not follow the crowd he won't complain of those who do.
> Rank and reward make no appeal to him; disgrace and shame do not deter him. He is not always looking for

right and wrong, always deciding "yes" or "no." The ancients said, therefore, "The Man of Tao remains unknown. Perfect virtue produces nothing. 'No-self' is true self. And the greatest man is nobody."

One of the problems we have with meditation is that we're afraid to meet ourselves and to meet God. In meditation, we think that going within ourselves will be uncomfortable. That's because we fear and doubt ourselves, and are quite sure that God doesn't like us either. Surrendering to that fear and meditating anyway is the sure, powerful way to begin to lick that problem. The control I see people attempt to exercise in meditation comes out of that fear. "If I don't control this meditation process look what I might find! Inside I might be the most god-awful mess since Fibber McGee's closet." My experience is the opposite. When we meditate we find our God who loves us as we are.

There was an interesting piece of research done called "Management by Mantra." Teams of business students were given a set of complex problems to solve. After solving these problems for an hour, one group was told about meditation and what a good thing it was. The other group had meditation explained to them and then meditated for about a half an hour. After this they were all given some more problems to solve. The group that meditated a half an hour was 30 percent more effective in the second hour of problem solving.

Meditation has meant so much to me. It has done so much for me. Many people come to me and say, "I'd like to have more peace of mind, Jess." And I say to them "meditate." They answer in one way or another, "I don't want to take the time to do that. Tell me something else I can do."

I've seen, when I see something someone else is doing that is of obvious benefit to them, that I should try it if I want what I see they have. I've seen that when I've found something good, I'm smart to hang on to it and use it.

A man came up to Bankei the great Zen master. This man was a priest of another sect, and he said to Bankei, "I only obey those I respect. I don't respect you, so I won't obey you." Bankei said to him, "Why, you're obviously a very intelligent man. Won't you come up and sit closer to me so I can talk to you."

The man came closer. Bankei said, "Here sit on my left," and the man sat down. Bankei said, "On second thought, come and sit over here on my right so that I can hear you better." The man moved over on Bankei's right. Bankei then said, "See. You're obeying me already. I can see that you are a very gentle, kind man. Why don't you sit here and learn about Zen."

There didn't use to be any respect or any obedience in me. I know how much that cost me. When we won't respect anything and won't obey we are like proud, angry children. When we remain proud, angry children we pay an awful price.

It takes ten years to be a Zen master. One day a young man finished his study and became a master. He was very excited about this and went to see Hakkim, a very old and respected Zen master. It was raining, and as he entered Hakkim's house he left his umbrella and slippers at the door. He was ushered into the great Zen master's presence and Hakkim greeted him and then said, "When you entered my house, on which side of your slippers did you place your umbrella?" The young Zen master saw that he could not tell Hakkim. He immediately renounced his new Zen mastership and began to study for three more years under Hakkim because he realized that he could not practice "every-minute Zen."

Meditation teaches us to be every minute where we are. When we live in the present moment we are better able to handle what happens in those moments. This enables us to cope in a better way with life. It helps us to understand the flow of life and to see that fortune and misfortune are all the same. It stops us from feeling that the arrows that land in our butt were aimed just at us. It stops us from sticking our butt in the path of the arrows and then when one lands, screaming and crying.

What I would suggest to you is that you try meditation for thirty days. I say this for only one reason—it works. I've never seen anyone who really tried it who did not get some results. The only limitation I see is your devotion to it.

Muktananda has a lot of Americans who go to his ashram in India when he is there. After meditation time many people share what happened to them in their meditations. Afterward some of the natives of India came to Muktananda and told him that they didn't understand why so many of the Americans had such vivid and enjoyable meditations. Muktananda said, "Do you meditate regularly?" The Indians said, "Well, no." "The Americans do," he replied.

You know, God makes the potatoes grow, but we have to plant and hoe them.

I will explain the way I meditate to you. Read it all and then try it for twenty minutes to an hour. I recommend that you do this in the morning. I know that you will probably have to get up a little earlier, but that won't kill you. Have a cup of tea if you want, but don't have breakfast first. It's best not to meditate on a full stomach.

There are four crucial parts to meditation: 1. Have the intent to meet God. 2. Use some word or words to concentrate on to still your mind. 3. Sit in a posture that facilitates meditation and use that same posture, time, and place of meditation as much as possible. 4. Concentrate on your breathing.

Sit in a comfortable chair. Sit upright with your feet flat on the floor and your hands relaxed in your lap. Hold your head up straight and your chin in. The mantra we will use is "ham-so." "Ham" is close to the sound of the incoming breath. "So" is close to the sound of the outgoing breath. You want to have your spine straight and your neck holding your head upright but in a relaxed way. Take a couple of deep breaths first and relax as much as you can.

Close your eyes and as you breathe in say silently to yourself, "Ham." As you expel your breath, say to yourself, "So." And that's it. "Ham-so." At the point of stillness within you where your incoming breath stops and just before the outgoing breath, there is God within. At the point of stillness without where your breath stops, there is God also. God within and God without, it's the same God. Remember this is your God, the God of your understanding. As you continue on with your eyes closed saying "ham-so" with each incoming and outgoing breath let any thoughts that you may have just flow on through. They are not important. The minute you are aware that you are thinking of something or experiencing anything return to your mantra—"ham-so." If a fire engine goes by the house, don't dwell on it, just keep your eyes closed, and the minute you are aware of the noise return to saying "ham-so." Do the same with any noise. If the baby starts to cry, use common sense. If it needs attending

to, don't try to stay in meditation. Meditate when it is not likely
that you will be disturbed.

If you become curious about the length of time you have been
meditating just gently open your eyes and look at your watch.
Then close your eyes and return to "ham-so." If you have an
itch, just scratch it but keep your eyes closed and continue with
your mantra.

Usually, your inward clock will let you know when you have
meditated as long as you planned. You may think you have
meditated long enough, but wait until you're sure of it. That's
usually close to or the exact time you had planned to quit. Also,
with practice you'll find you come out of meditation at the set
time.

When you wish to stop meditating, keep your eyes closed but
slowly reach your arms up over your head and give a big
stretch. Sit quietly for a minute and then get up and go about
your day.

If you wish further aids to meditation I recommend the book,
Meditate by Baba Muktananda.[1] And also his book entitled *I Am
That*.[2]

My friend Wally Minto has tapes on meditation. You can
write to him at Alpha Awareness, Drawer G., Susanville, California. His tapes are excellent. My wife, Jackie, also has a tape to
guide you into meditation. She has used this technique in guiding groups at our seminars and at our schools. You can write to
me at P. O. Box 249, Bozeman, Montana, for that tape.

Our minds make us dance like a monkey. The whole point of
meditation is clearing away the fictions of the mind and being
an observer to that mind and that takes away the power of the
mind. It has been said, "The mind is a wonderful slave but a
terrible master."

The whole point of this book is that we go to the deep, inner
part of ourselves, without the mind, and find the sense of wholeness and the intuitive direction for ourselves that is beyond
words and beyond concepts. The closest to putting it in words is
that we become "no-thing," nothing special.

[1] State University of New York Press, State University Plaza, Albany, NY
12246. $3.95 plus postage.
[2] SYDA Foundation, P. O. Box 605, South Fallsburg, NY 12779. $3.50 plus
postage.

This is the point made by the quote from *Chuang Tzu* about the Man of Tao. It is also the point made by many quotes in the Bible, like the quotation about "who by thinking can increase his stature by a single cubit." Or the story of the people who were invited to the wedding banquet and went. Or the people who came into the vineyard at the last hour and were paid the same as those who came first.

Sure there are ideas and inspirations that come to us while in meditation. They can give valuable direction to our lives. When I'm working on a book, I get valuable insights and material that provides direction and ideas for the book. That's fine. I receive these things gratefully. They will come as they are needed. But I always keep in mind that what counts most is to continue to keep my mind out of the driver's seat so that anything that wants to come can.

If I'm to have blackness, beautiful. If I'm to have deep visions and experiences of God, beautiful. I sit in the sure knowledge that what I need, God will bring me. This even includes new concepts of meditation itself. I can't be fixed on anything except my trust that God will provide me just exactly what I need. The means, methods, and channels through which God will provide that are up to God. I don't want my conscious mind to have much say-so in the matter because it has so often been the trickster and the deluder. The point is that my mind be in balance with the other parts of me so those parts can all work in harmony. But my mind wants to be the dictator, as it has in the past, demanding complete control. Then, when its control produces ashes in my life, it justifies itself and says, "You didn't give me enough control. Give me more control and then I will work for you."

That is the same message the whiskey bottle gives to the alcoholic. "I know I didn't solve all of your problems yesterday, but just take more or less of me in some certain way and I will work those wonders for you that you seek." It takes a long time for the alcoholic to see that the bottle doesn't have the answers he seeks.

In the same way it's taken me a long time to see that my mind doesn't have the answers. It's a valuable part of me. It's great at solving crossword puzzles and calculus problems, but it can't run my life and have the complete control as it insists. My mind has to give up its demand for absolute control and take its proper place in the harmony of body, mind and spirit all working together in often mysterious ways for my higher good.

Meditation can't be learned from a book. I'm giving you enough about meditation so you can have a clearer sense of what I'm talking about. But I believe that you need to really experience meditation for yourself to find out what I'm talking about. Put these ideas to work as well as you can. And then look at the resources available to you and reach out for the help you need. Send for tapes. Find someone who meditates to teach you. Take the TM course. Go to a Muktananda ashram or one of the many Siddha Yoga centers that have been set up around the country. They have free meditation classes and they are not seeking converts.

Someone asked Muktananda if he was trying to get people to leave their religions. He said, "No. I'm trying to help people be better practitioners of the religions they have. I'm trying to help people to feel God inside them; to wake up. What religion is being asleep a part of?"

Don't worry that your God is so weak that by walking into an ashram, you'll lose him. Your God is a strong God, one with all power, and he wants the best for you whether you understand that or not. So your God will guide you to deeper experiences of God that are in your framework of understanding.

One of the reasons I think meditation works so powerfully is that when we sit down to meditate we are overthrowing the tyranny of the mind and saying to the spirit, "This is your time to have your place in the sun. We are sitting still to quiet our body. We are closing our eyes to still the stimuli that stir the mind so you, the spirit can play your part and lead us to wholeness." Meditation turns off the body and the mind so we can be moved by the spirit and listen to the spirit if, and when, it has something that needs to be said. But we must understand that there isn't anything that needs to be said.

If we will understand that meditation's usefulness is primarily to unite our scattered and fragmented being, it will help us to avoid putting so much emphasis on God speaking to us or us trying to concentrate on what we think are holy things. We aren't in charge of deciding what's holy, that's God's business.

I remember not too many years ago when I constantly seeking

"guidance." I would be wondering if my role was to restore peace in South Africa, heal the sick, or build a cathedral someplace. Then I realized that my work was right in front of me lying undone. My work was to pull the weeds in my garden.

What a shock that was at first to have to come off my holy high horse, me, the savior of the world. But then I was relieved. This frightened little boy was staggered by the idea of having to move the world. But there was no need for me to be frightened by pulling weeds. I could do that. Even though my own garden was suffering from years of neglect, I could still pull the weeds and gradually clean up my garden. Once my garden was clean it was so simple to keep it that way. And, if I missed a weed that was too small to see it was simple, because the weed would get bigger and become more obvious, and I could get it then.

Meditation played a big part in making me more whole and giving me the calmness to see my work. More and more I see that I don't need guidance. My work is right in front of me waiting to be picked up and done.

But always the enemy is my mind. It wants obvious "holy" thoughts and grandiose jobs. Instead, what God does is calm me down so I can see what's in front of me in my daily life with Jackie, with my family, with my work, with my horses, and with all the rest of my life.

Another way the mind crops up in meditation is in greediness for the spectacular meditation. Others describe meditations full of beautiful visions, seeing God, the blue lights, and on and on. I want what they have. That's spiritual materialism. I don't need those things from God. If I needed them for me, I would have them. What God is doing for me is giving me what I need when I need it, which right now is more wholeness and peace and clarity of vision. Those are beautiful gifts, maybe so beautiful that you're seeing the blue lights and envying me the fruits of my meditation. So my meditation will yield what's right for me.

Meditation is God's time to do just exactly as he chooses. I continually suffer from ego and think some things are high and some low. I think I should have visions of God and walk in holy places. But what God wants me to do is fix the screen door that's been busted for two years.

God has equal vision. I don't. God sees a pile of horse manure and a pile of gold as the same; both physical manifestations of

God. I see them as different. That's my problem. It's what I have to get rid of. It's what I have to guard against in meditation so I don't try to structure meditation so it produces what I think is holy.

Also, in meditation, I need to rest in God. I'm the one who is continually feeling the need to do something. God is content with his handiwork. I'm continually wanting to change his picture, to improve on his handiwork, to change the things I can't understand and can't see that are a part of God and God's love. So in meditation I need to be open to God and throw away my judging, discriminating mind to be ready for what is there for me and not to seek what is not there and what I don't need.

In the introduction to *I Am That*, Swami Prajnananda quotes from the Essene Gospel of Peace, Book Two. This was from Jesus' time, and some ascribe the words to Jesus. "We worship the Holy Breath which is placed higher than all the other things created. For, lo, the eternal and sovereign luminous space where rule the unnumbered stars, is the air we breathe in and breathe out. And in the moment betwixt the breathing in and breathing out is hidden all the mysteries of the Infinite Garden."

Muktananda says that mind and breath are twin brothers. What happens to one happens to the other. If one is controlled, the other is automatically controlled. Therefore, one of the methods of stilling the mind is to control the breathing.

Unevenness in breathing creates restlessness in the mind, and then the person sees the world as divided instead of as a single reflection of God.

When the mantra helps the breathing slow down and become more even, the mind becomes more balanced and quiet and God is seen everywhere, within and without.

So that is the function of focusing on the breathing. There are many ways to do this. In Zen the breathing is counted. The Hindus use their mantras. As I said, the mantra I use is "ham-so" on the incoming and outgoing breath. The point I see as important is not some magic in words but it is the result that counts. "Ham-so" means "I am that." If anything Eastern makes you uncomfortable or suspicious, use a word or words that are meaningful to you to accomplish the same purpose, or count your breaths, which is free of any religious association.

For a word in your meditation, you could use Jesus, splitting the name saying "Je" on the incoming breath and "sus" on the outgoing. I tried other Christian words as aids. One I used was "praise God." That didn't seem to work as well because "God" is a word that ends with a consonant that is shut off rather than drawn out as is the "e" in "Je" and the "s" in "sus." I don't know if that's important or not, but it seemed to me not to fit in with the breathing as well. But in counting, many of the numbers don't end in soft, drawn-out vowel or consonant sounds either. The big point is, don't get hung up on words, find something that suits you and use it to see if it works for you.

So many people have their theology so well worked out and figured out that they know all the answers to everything and there are no questions their minds aren't made up on. They can give you a well thought out and scripturally sound argument on everything.

That may be fine for them, but I see theology in a different way than they do. I see God's word as a guide to me rather than a set of answers. Since I'm a limited, finite human being, I'll never see that guidance and that way perfectly clearly. There will always be areas of mystery, things I can't reconcile or figure out. But that element of mystery I can handle. In fact, I'm reassured by it. You see, if I can figure out God, I am God. If I can understand God, I have God scaled down to the limits of my human mind, and that would scare me. I want and need a much bigger God than one I can understand with my mind. I need a God who has all power and works in all things. Just how God can manage this I can't figure out and don't want to try.

My mind is what I'm trying to overcome because it wants absolute rule. When my mind says to me, "Jess, even talking about breathing isn't Christian, it's from those weird Eastern gods," the best I can do is come back and say, "That's fine, but the crucial part of creation was when God breathed life into Adam." And we know from their writings that many of the early mystical Christians used meditation techniques. Yet I've given a few seminars for leaders of religious groups, and when I talk to them about this kind of meditation, I'm talking about something that's new and strange to most of them.

When I ask myself why this is, the best answer I can find is that we live in what we call an "Age of Reason." It has been a long time since we first lifted the mind up and glorified it so.

Even in the Charismatic and Pentecostal movements, where people are seeking the spiritual so avidly, I see so much emphasis on words and thinking.

Thomas Wolfe in one of his books talked about the brain and its absolutism so beautifully. He said something to the effect of, "What is it that tells us the brain is so smart? It is the brain that tells us the brain is so smart." So the brain defines and evaluates itself. This is the tyranny of the mind. And, to me, this is the predominant thread that runs through Western civilization.

The great mind will do it all. If the mind isn't solving a problem or is getting us in trouble, we don't think of looking someplace else for the answer. We just say to the mind, "Work harder," and the mind says to us, "Your problems are coming because you don't depend on me enough." It never occurs to us that the great big mind that we are looking to for answers and solutions is the problem.

But I tell you I'm convinced. I've got a fine mind, but my mind and I got into a lot of trouble. So I give up on that absolute dictatorship of the mind. I seek a balance between my spirit, mind, and body where the spirit is the leader and the three parts are in total harmony.

Here is where meditation is so necessary to me. It is the means by which I give the spirit time to work in my life, time to heal me, make me more whole, and give me any little guidance I need.

But the dictatorship of the mind is not easily overthrown. To me, that explains why meditation doesn't immediately become a big part of my life. But I see what meditation does for me by giving the spirit its time in the sun and leading me to the experience of wholeness. So most every morning you'll find me spending some time sitting still with my eyes shut saying "ham-so."

If you're put off by this talk of meditation as something that seems very strange and foreign to you, think of it as learning to kiss. All of us learned to kiss by jumping in and just starting. There were no books to read, no teachers to tell us how, we just did it. We got better, and the teaching we needed came naturally. Same with meditation. Just start in right now with what I've told you and anything else you know. You'll learn it as you did kissing. You may not ever be great at it in your eyes, but the job will get done. Good luck.

Chapter Three

LOVE—THAT'S ALL THERE IS

The understanding of God and love that is most helpful to me is one I got from reading a report of the final spiritual realization of a great saint. He saw a vision where the radiance of God was like the sun and the rays of the sun shot out and became all the individual beings and objects we see in the world. God was in the center of the sun, then his teacher was in the center of the sun, and then the saint was in the center of the sun. He experienced that everything was God and love. God was in him and he was in God. The whole world was simply the play of God, the sport of God. Since then he sees God first and then the individual. The whole world is bathed in the blue light of God.

We limited ones see distinctions. We see ourselves as separate from God and other people. But as Earnie Forks of the Church of Religious Science says, "It's just one." There is just one thing. That one thing is love in its many, many forms. None of us is able to grasp this, but love is the system. The essence of every human being and every other animate and inanimate thing here on this earth is love.

In order to begin to grasp this fact we must throw out all of our old ideas. Our old ideas are the things that are crippling us. The idea that the essence of everything is love is a very useful idea. It makes more sense than the ideas that brought us to the neurosis and negativity most of us are crippled with today.

Most of the ideas we choose to believe in and hang on to are all ego-centered ideas. They are ideas that bring us into judgment; this is right, that is wrong, my way is right, yours isn't. Negativity, negativity; all around us negativity. Baba Muktananda asks one thing. He says, "Give me your negativity." I would say the same thing. I would also say, "Give me your judgmental attitudes." Put them down. Those attitudes were what convinced you that you were not good enough, and those attitudes made your mind your master instead of your servant. Your judgmental attitudes rig the game of life against you, they close your mind and keep you locked into your negativity.

I have an old friend who came into Alcoholics Anonymous off skid row. At the same time that my friend was sobering up, alongside of him was another man sobering up who was a Ph.D. in theology from Notre Dame. This man's family was paying him $400 a month to stay out of Cook County, Illinois. They were sick and tired of his passing bad checks on their friends and embarrassing them with his crazy behavior. When my old friend started coming to the spiritual part of Alcoholics Anonymous he said to this Ph.D., "Boy, when it comes to the spiritual part of this program you've really got the advantage with your tremendous education in theology." The Ph.D. said, "No. It's exactly the opposite. My mind is so full of things that ain't so; so full of false beliefs, that I have ten times the problem you've got. I've got so much garbage to get rid of."

Many, many people have religious beliefs that are based on superstitious nonsense. Their beliefs are not only against scripture, they are against the Christ-idea, which is love. Many of you could go to a blackboard for me and write, without coercion, one hundred times, "I believe that I am a part of God and God is a part of me." I could tell you that I didn't want you to do it unless you truly believed it, and you could say, "I truly believe it." You'd write it one hundred times and still nothing would happen. Why? Because until you have experienced this, it is only a head trip, an intellectual exercise.

I don't debate religion with anyone. Everyone is entitled to his own beliefs; to believe in God as he understands him. I have left the debating society and moved more and more toward the principles in the twelve-step groups, like Emotions Anonymous and Alcoholics Anonymous, that offer the freedom of each of us seeing God as we understand him and so encourage our growth toward an ever-deeper spirituality, the essence of which is love.

My mind is too finite to be able to understand that God is love when I don't experience love from my fellow man. And love is an experience, not an intellectual exercise. I think this is what

Jesus was saying to us when he said, "How can you say you love God, whom you have not seen, when you do not love your neighbor, whom you have seen?"

Love is the perfect tool, perfect in everyway. We keep throwing this tool away and going over and picking up the rusty old tools of judgment and negativity that the egos of mankind have been using from generation to generation for thousands of years.

Why do we throw away God-given tools? Simple. We throw them away because we don't know what they are. We live in our delusions and illusions filled with pain and fear and anger at our terrible human dilemma because staying with what we know seems safer than the risk of opening our minds. We're afraid. The one thing my puny little ego can't stand is to be wrong. I'd rather be right than be President, even if it kills me.

In this chapter on love, I'm sharing with you what love is to me now. As with all of my books I'm just sharing my journey, my trip through life. In my earlier books I told you about acceptance. I told you how I felt when I walked into a room full of people who accepted me just as I am. I told you how being accepted like that helped me to accept myself. I told you how ". . . when we accept ourselves as we are, then we can change."

I had to recognize my own neurosis. I had to recognize what a powerful God-given tool I had in the knowledge that "the essence of everything is love." And I had to see that every time I threw away the clean perfect tools of love and picked up the tools of my old beliefs I was crazy. It's crazy to throw away perfect tools and go over and pick up my old rusty toolbox half filled with old rusty tools. It's crazy. I know I'm crazy when I do it, but I do it anyway. And that's the problem.

All right. We all know that God is love and that we are a part of God and God is a part of us, so why don't we act like it? That's because love is an experience, it's not something we know. We all say, "I'm not stupid, Jess, I know that." I thought I knew that too. But the knowing is not enough. It is the experience of this that counts. But how do we experience it?

First of all we have to see that we are trapped on the horns of a dilemma. We have been like Diogenes who roamed the world seeking an honest man. We roam the world seeking love, and yet all the love we need is right inside of us. But it seems that at first, when we're beginners at loving, we can't recognize that love unless we see it reflected in other people's love. And so it takes a miracle. But miracles are all around us, they're happening every day if we're open to them.

I've seen these miracles in Alcoholics Anonymous or Emotions Anonymous, or other spiritual groups. I've seen people whose own mothers and fathers have given up on them, experience God's love for them through the warmth and acceptance of the people in these groups. They are people who have been given up on by doctors and priests and psychiatrists and psychologists and ministers and every do-gooder in the world. But finally these hurting people come to these groups, usually as their last resort, and experience what they need and have sought so desperately all of their lives. I've watched their amazement as they look at a room full of crazy people just like them and say, "What's wrong? I'm getting what I've always wanted. How come? What's wrong?" I've watched their crazy minds start looking for reasons. And then, what's even worse, I've watched them challenge the love of the group. I've watched the alcoholic or neurotic go into their crazy act and seen their dismay when this doesn't affect the group's love for them. And slowly, if they can stand the love and stay around, I've watched the miracle of love transform these derelicts into beautiful, productive, outgoing human beings.

Now, I guess I'd have to say in all humility that I was crazier than they were. I watched this miracle going on for years. I tasted some of it myself. But I did not truly experience it for myself in a deep overwhelming way until I went to Muktananda's ashram in Florida. And I have to ask, "Why?" The answer as I see it, is humility. We can't find what we seek or experience it fully unless we are finally driven to it. Humility is the name of that game. We finally have to have the humility to say, "I don't know. I can't do it for myself." We have to finally cry out for help. Then the teachers who are waiting to teach us will appear. In most cases they were at our elbow all the time, but we were so full of "I can do it myself, Mother," that we couldn't see them.

I finally know what makes me such a good teacher. It isn't my brilliance. It's my stubbornness and persistence in pursuing my old ways. Life has continually dealt me hands that made me seek answers or go crazy or die or some other negative thing like that. Life never let me have a softer, easier way, and I have to say now, "Thank God for that."

In Florida, in the atmosphere of Muktananda's ashram, I experienced overwhelming love. Notice I say *"experienced."* We've all talked about love. We've all had people say that they love us, and we've all told people that we love them, but most of the time when they tell us they love us, we don't feel much of anything, and that really hurts. We've all had it up to here with talking about something and not feeling anything. It's enough to drive us all crazy or to drink or to a premature grave.

So what was it I experienced in Florida? I experienced the essence of a "God-realized" man. What is the essence of a God-realized man? The essence is love, a love so powerful that it is a perfect mirror to me of my own essence. What is my own essence? It too is love. The same love that is in Baba Muktananda. The same essence that is in Jesus Christ.

So, what did I learn from this "God-realized" man whose essence is a love more powerful than any I've ever experienced? I learned that the essence of everything is pure love. I learned that when I don't feel love it is because I am seeking it in the wrong places. I cannot find love in my wife or my children or my friends or my horses or my town unless I carry it around with me. The first love I have to know is my own love.

"What?" you say. I'll say it again another way. The only love Jackie will ever really know is her own love. The only love my kids will ever really know is their own love. They can't do it for me and I can't do it for them. That's where so much of our human dilemma lies. Our human dilemma is really our life's journey back to God, back to love, back to our essence, to whatever degree we are capable of.

At every turn, from earliest childhood, we have been taught and trained to look outward for what we need. This belief is in the very air we breathe. So many of us believe or have believed that the reason we are the way we are is because "Mama or Daddy didn't love us enough." Well, they did love us. We got the exact measure of love we needed to sustain our lives, and any more than that was a divine gift to us. All we needed or deserved was enough love to sustain our lives, and the rest is up to us. That's what life is all about.

From the time we were very small we chose what we would

believe and what we would not, and if we are shipwrecked now, we have to accept responsibility for that. This idea—that we are responsible—is the only idea that will work for us. If we say that we cannot love ourselves because Mama and Daddy didn't love us enough, then we can't find what we seek, can we? We can't make anyone love us. When we believe that what we are today is others' responsibility, then only others can give us what we need. That's the belief that something outside ourselves has the answer. Only others can save us. That belief is an old rusty tool. For me it doesn't work.

In the old days people used to believe that the sun revolved around the earth. The only problem was that they could not come up with an astronomy that worked, believing that way. They could make no predictions that were valid from that belief. But that belief was held valid for thousands of years. Their egos demanded that they were the center and the sun revolved around them. They couldn't imagine it any other way. Finally, an astronomer realized that the earth revolved around the sun. This idea was horrible and repugnant to the people and almost got the astronomer killed. But that belief worked. With that belief you could make predictions that were valid. So truth is what works—in astronomy, in physics, and in life.

As I mentioned earlier, one day at the ashram in Florida, I was walking alone and barefoot on a sandy beach looking for seashells. All of a sudden I realized I was feeling overwhelming love. I experienced that I was love. I was feeling love because I was in contact with my own essence, which is love. Then I knew that I was experiencing a small measure of God-realization. Because Muktananda lives so close to his essence he was able to communicate the essence of my own love to me without touching me or holding me or even telling me. His essence is so powerful it awakened my essence.

I used to think, when I held Jackie, that any love I felt came from her. Or even worse, I used to feel that any lack of my feeling love came from her also. Now the interesting thing is Jackie agrees with me. She came to this knowledge and belief, not through Muktananda or through me, but through experiencing the essence of another human being whom she calls "The Idiot of Bernbach." She has written a small book about him. We each experienced the same knowledge, thousands of miles apart, at different times and in different places and in different ways. We each, in our own individual way, were humbled enough to be taught by the teachers whom we were given. And our experiences were each unique to our individual personalities, yet the truth that evolved from these very different teachers and very different ways was the same truth.

I firmly believe that every human being on this earth has teachers waiting to teach them. But most of you are just like us. It was only our stubbornness and our fear and our clinging to old ways that kept us from learning for so very long.

We all want to say that we must be loved by certain someones, and if those certain someones didn't love us or don't love us, we can't be loved. And so those certain someones have the power of life and death over us.

I've observed people in their fifties and sixties living crabbed, mean, narrow existences because "their parents didn't love them enough." Their parents' bodies have long since moldered into dust, and their cases are hopeless, but they still persist in this delusion. So, for them the world is rotten, people are no damn good, and there is no God. Well, what are the fruits of all of that negativity? You can see it on their faces, just look.

You see those same sour faces on many so-called religious people who see God as a vengeful, terrifying God who will not love them unless they do "good." Doing good consists of their deciding what's right and what's wrong, what's good and what's bad, and then deciding who is "us" and who is "those others." And by their fruits you know them, too. There doesn't seem to be any love for themselves or any others in a barrelful of them.

These kinds of people used to terrify me. Now I know that the essence of them is love. The more I can be in touch with my own essence, the more clearly I become a mirror to them of their own love. I must put down my negativity and judgmental attitude toward them. They have their trip and I have mine. More and more now, I am having the experience of smiling at some person who appears sad or crabby, and they break into a smile.

When we suddenly see and understand that the essence of each of us is love and the essence of every other person and every other thing on earth is love too, how does this affect us? First of all we feel relief, a great overwhelming relief. When I believed that my love came from Jackie and my kids and my friends and from some nebulous God who gave it to me when I got a gold star on my chart, I was at the mercy of everyone. When we believe that old way, we are like puppy dogs with our tongues hanging out, always ready to roll over and do any trick we know to get a crumb of love. When we blame everyone else for our lack of love, we starve to death at a banquet table because we wait for it to be served to us instead of taking what is there for us.

Even when we see the truth we still try to deny it. We try to deny it because we don't want to be responsible. We avoid taking responsibility for our own lives because most of us weren't taught this kind of responsibility. How could we be taught it? Our parents and our teachers and our ministers didn't know it either. A crucial part of taking responsibility for ourselves is looking honestly at ourselves so we can see we put ourselves in our own prison. We made the choices that brought us here. It takes the deepest kind of self-honesty to see this. To get this self-honesty and to increase it, we need to be around people who are honest with themselves too. That's why a continuing contact with a growth group of some kind is so necessary. A group can't facilitate growth unless the members practice self-honesty.

Most people think of honesty as cash-register honesty. I don't steal and I don't tell lies, at least nothing more than a few small white lies. But that's not the most important honesty which is self-honesty. When we get a steadily increasing measure of self-honesty we can become aware of our choices and their consequences. We can begin to see the costs of our babyishness and irresponsibility. Most people are very responsible about paying their bills and running a business. Those same people can be the biggest irresponsible babies in the world in their personal lives. It's hard to face how irresponsible we have been. But we have to see we have choices and we're making them all the time. When we choose to say we don't have a choice, that's a choice—and a very dangerous one.

It's an awesome terrible thing for us to have to face the fact that we created our own reality. We created our own lack of love. We created our own limited concept of God, and furthermore we used this because it served our needs to be judgmental and critical and ego-centered and to create a limited world of "us and them." We thought that way was easier than recognizing that we are all one and that the oneness is love, and that love is the essence of everyone and everything. Believing this new way takes a new understanding and a new awareness. We still are a lot like those people hundreds of centuries ago whose egos demanded that the sun revolve around them, even when that belief didn't give them any tools to work with to make their lives on this earth a little better.

To experience love, to know love, we have to walk our own walk. We all say, "I can't do it. I don't know how. It won't work" —or a thousand variations of this, all trying to convince ourselves that we don't know what we have to do. To all of this I just have to say that deep within yourself you do know what you have to do.

Our attitudes remind me of a story that Stephen Gaskin of The Farm in Summertown, Tennessee, tells. Stephen says that when God gave Moses the Ten Commandments, God knew Moses and his people would soon want to start arguing with God, saying that they didn't know just how to follow each commandment. So God then gave Moses an eleventh commandment. It was, "You do, too, know what I mean." Of course, we all know exactly what is going on within us and around us all the time. We just like to pretend we don't. That's our game. It enables us to continue to avoid responsibility.

The belief that I carry love inside of me, and when I hold Jackie it is my own love that is awakened sounds like a very pat explanation. That is immaterial as I see it. It's an idea that works for me. If it works for me, it is true. The reason this idea is so powerful is because it focuses me on my own part in the transaction and doesn't put the responsibility on her.

I once heard an explanation of marriage. "Marriage is taking two neurotics and leaning them up against each other." The only thing is, this doesn't work too well. Look at our divorce rate. The problem in marriage is that we marry someone in the false belief that they will fulfill our needs. This is all part of the syndrome, the belief, that something or someone outside ourselves can give us what we need, what we seek. And of course, this never works. So most of us think the divorce court is the answer. It isn't just the present generation either. People who've been married thirty and forty years are splitting up today as never before.

Well, where is all of this coming from? I think it's coming from our irresponsibility, our lack of commitment, our false belief that if there is pain anywhere, in our body, in our mind, or our puny little egos, we've got to get rid of it as fast as we can. We've become a world of sissies, of cowards who will not accept pain or even death in our lives. We have to begin somewhere, and that somewhere has to be with us. We have to stop looking at our wives or our husbands or our kids and wishing they would change so we could feel better. That way doesn't work.

I learned a lot about myself at the ashram. I began to see myself thinking negatively. I would look at someone and think, "Isn't he crabby? Aren't they uptight? Aren't they negative?" As I recognized what I was doing I found a way out. The minute I was aware of what I was doing I would think, "Hey, there is love, there is love."

I wasn't home more than a few weeks when I went to a horsemanship school in Bozeman. The school's run by a man who has become a good friend of mine named Ray Hunt. He's teaching the same ideas for horses that I'm trying to understand. He looks like an everyday cowboy, but he's really a saint in disguise. That's the way of this world. Many things aren't the way they seem to be. Ray's pretending to teach us how to be kind to our horses, but he's actually teaching us how to be kind to our wives.

Most of us think the way we stop a horse is to pull back hard on the reins. Right? Wrong! The way to stop a horse is to hold the reins as if you are holding a hummingbird with a thread. Then you pay attention to your horse's feet. As she is in mid-stride you gently indicate by a slight pull on the reins that you would like her to stop. You invite your horse to stop. Your horse feels your invitation, puts her foot down and then knows that her next stride will be her last. You give her momentum a chance to slow up, you see. And you do it intelligently, paying attention to your horse. If I can do this for my horse, wouldn't you think that I could be as gentle with my wife?

Well, at this school I was listening to Ray, but I was also gazing at the back of a lady in front of me. I was thinking, "She's got a butt that must be an ax-handle wide. What a fatty." I realized to my horror what I was thinking and switched my thoughts to "Love, there is love." In a few minutes she rode over to me and started to talk to me. What had happened you see is, as I got rid of my negativity I was all of a sudden, approachable. No way would she come up to me when I was concentrating on the fact that her butt was as wide as an ax handle. If she had, she would have really been stupid. But she wasn't that blind. She was able to sense my new, changed attitude even though she didn't know me or what I was thinking.

More and more I'm experiencing that all of the separation I feel in my life is artificial. It is a fiction that I maintain with great effort on my part. All around me I see there is great pain in our lives as we feel the consequences of feeling separate and alone. But we believe in separation, we vigorously maintain it, and then we wonder how come we hurt so bad.

I had to recognize that I had a life-long habit of looking critically at other people and of thinking critically about other people. In the beginning perhaps this negative habit developed as the only way I could make my puny little ego feel good, feel important. Perhaps I needed to look down on people. The consequences of that habit were isolation. I drove away even the people I thought I loved with this attitude, this habit. I suffered pain, but I stoutly maintained that I saw these negative things in them because of them, not me. Now I see that I created that reality.

As I've gotten a deeper understanding of the fact that I am love and that I'm a part of God and that God's a part of me, a funny thing has happened. I've come to realize more and more that I'm no big thing. And my little ego that was so tender is now able to stand more truth about myself.

I was talking to a friend of mine about these ideas and my friend said, "Gee, Jess. You make me feel like I should go back and raise my kids a different way. I taught them to believe they were somebody, maybe I should have taught them they were nobody." In a sense this is true.

My wife and I were talking about this a few weeks ago, and Jackie said she never forgot a conversation she had with a friend of ours, Ruthie Harding, in Minneapolis over twenty years ago. They were discussing a mutual acquaintance who had just up and left her husband and children. Ruthie said to Jackie, "I'd always noticed something about her, Jackie. She was so physically beautiful that she spent her whole life getting by on her beauty. She never had to learn to give and take."

It's crucial for everyone to realize that they are *nobody special*. And to accept that fact. We all run around with our inferiority complexes, which really are superiority complexes. We only feel inferior to our own grandiose idea that we should be *somebody*. The sad thing is that our ego is never satisfied, and no matter how rich or how famous or how beautiful we are it's never good enough when you live with the belief that you've got to be *somebody*. Ask a millionaire if he's rich enough. Ask a movie star if she's pretty enough. Ask a model if she's thin enough. They'll all say, "NO."

I was talking to someone recently and the old quote attributed to Joe Lewis came up. "I've been rich and I've been poor, and rich is best." My wife laughed and said, "Well, I've been rich and I've been poor and I don't see any difference." This is true, right down to absolute starvation-level poverty. There are people dying of starvation with more peace and joy and love in their lives than can be found in some of the wealthier homes in the world. I'm not saying poor is the answer. I'm saying rich, poor; fat, thin; beautiful, ugly; it's all the same. There are Yogis in India so immersed in their essence, which is love, that they have lived for years on a cup of milk a day and nothing else.

Here in the Western world there are people that my wife and I know personally who are in touch with their essence to the degree that they can eat whatever they want, whenever they want, and they never gain or lose weight or suffer any ill health. We know people who have quit smoking without withdrawal symptoms or weight gain when their attitude changed toward who they were.

The most startling paradox in the world is that the deeper we go into our essence and the deeper we realize that we are truly nothing special, the more special we become. The more we are able to see that our ego and how it is handled is not important, the more we can become that fantastically unique person we were created to be.

When we know we are nothing special we are open to the world around us and to our teachers. When we know we are nothing special we become true learners. We lose our big fat egos that have to be handled with kid gloves. I am nothing special!

Suzuki wrote the great book *Zen Mind, Beginner's Mind*. In this book he points out that to the beginner life is full of possibilities; life is rich and varied. Once we consider that we are something special, an expert, we have very few possibilities. We have narrowed life down. We are full of opinions, and we are so busy evaluating and judging things that we never directly experience anything.

It's like the first time we rode a ferris wheel. Remember the delicious feeling of going up, up, up, and then down, down, and around? Remember the lights and how pretty they were? Remember looking out over the countryside and down at the people? Wonderful! But by our fiftieth ferris wheel ride; "Oh, just another ferris wheel." What we need to do is try to get to the point where we do everything for the first time, the beginner's mind where there are infinite possibilities. A necessary step toward this is to get rid of being an expert, get rid of all our opinions and see that "I'm nobody special."

In one of my earlier books I mentioned hearing a cowboy here in Bozeman say to another cowboy, "Let's have a drink and be somebody." Hearing that was so powerful to me. I've got a suspicion that cowboy really saw and understood that side of himself. To me, his statement is one of the most honest statements I've ever heard a human being make. A person doesn't have to be an alcoholic to recognize that alcohol does give us a glow, a good feeling inside that is based on a feeling of "being somebody." I'm learning that the same feeling, the same relaxed glow can come by just putting down the feeling that I'm somebody and recognizing that I'm nobody special.

The attitude that I'm nobody special is a powerful tool to help me live in the present moment. My wife, in her writing, has made the point that there is no pain in the present moment, that pain comes from living in the past or looking to the future. This is true to some extent. Right now, right here, at this very moment, there's nothing wrong. Nothing to fear. If we say, "Yes, but what about . . ." we are either looking back, or worrying ahead. If we pay deep attention to what has hurt us in the past or to what we worry about in the future, a lot of that pain comes from the expectations or disappointments of someone who thinks he's special. "This shouldn't happen to me. I deserve better than that. A person like me shouldn't have to deal with things like this."

Someone said to me, "Jess, isn't life kind of dull when you're living just in the moment, and it's just the same stuff over and over again?" And I said, "No, because beneath that seeming regularity and commonplace are the deepest kind of riches. It's like you've been sitting on a lake made muddy by the waves. All of a sudden the waves stop, the water clears, and you can look way below the surface. There are fish swimming beneath you and the weeds are waving gracefully below and the sun is glancing off of rocks way down deep. The beauty right below you is overwhelming. You had no idea it was there while the water was stirred and cloudy."

The present moment is vertical time. The past and the future is horizontal. Our minds can deal only with horizontal time. I believe love is found only in vertical time. We say, "I love you," we don't say, "I did love you," or "I will love you." We feel our essence, our love within us now, in this instant, or we never feel it. This is why I stress learning meditation. To me meditation is the only chance we have to teach our mind what the present moment is.

Our mind has been our master for all of our lives. But our mind cannot grasp or understand the present moment. Our mind is a tool, but we have given that tool too much power. We have been taught that our mind will set us free. We believed that and ignored the most powerful tool, which is experiencing our own essence—love. When we live in our mind we cannot experience. Our mind can define love. Our mind thinks; our mind cannot feel. Experience is feeling, which goes beyond the mind, the intellect. A whole person, a God-realized person, a saint, is a person who lives in the present moment, in their essence, using their mind as a tool to deal with anything that comes up in that moment.

A good way to help you see what power our minds have over us and how our minds can work to our pain and destruction is to tell you a story. A husband and wife sit down to breakfast. They've been married twenty-five years and the children, with all of their distractions, are gone. He's dressed for work, she's in her nightgown. He has his toast and corn flakes and orange juice. She has her coffee. They've done this practically every day for twenty-five years. It is the tenth of June and it's been raining and sleeting ever since Memorial Day. They aren't young anymore and the kids are gone and his corn flakes and her coffee are pretty old, tired, boring things.

He says to his wife, "Gee honey, I'm worried about the Smith account. It's the foundation of my business. Old man Smith has been pretty unpredictable lately and I don't know if Junior has the brains to run the business right. If something happens to old man Smith, I just don't know . . ."

What fires in the wife's mind? Old tapes! Instantly her brain feeds to her every time her husband has worried about the Smith account. And there are plenty of old tapes. He's been worrying about that account for twenty years, and nothing has ever happened to it. Her brain feeds her all these old tapes from the past. They run through her mind and she wants to say, "You big baby. You've been scaring hell out of me for twenty years now with your worry about that account, and nothing's happened. Why don't you grow up? Just quit chewing your boring corn flakes and go to work."

But she remembers that she loves her husband. Her brain tells her that too, and she bites her tongue and says, "That's too bad you're worried. It'll be all right. Gosh my hip hurts. I'm so sick and tired of all of the rain and cold."

And what happens in his brain? Old tapes! He thinks, "I'm worried about our financial future and she's complaining about the weather again. I've listened to her talk about her aches and pains for twenty years now, and I'm sick of it. Why doesn't she eat something healthy for breakfast instead of that damn coffee?" But his brain tells him that this is the woman that he loves and so he says, "That's too bad. I've got to go to work now."

They do love each other. They've lived in a committed relationship for twenty-five years now, and they have a lot of happy tapes stored in their brains as well. But the quality of that breakfast was lousy wasn't it? They didn't fool each other. Where did the negativity come from? His worry? Her hip? The rain? No. These are all legitimate things happening in the present moment. The negativity came from the mind which didn't deal with the single present moment but fed old tapes from its computer. Without the old tapes they each could have dealt compassionately with the other, treating each other's worry and pain lovingly, and felt better when they parted.

I believe that old tapes fired by our minds do more to kill love than anything else.

Old tapes are stored in our minds to teach us from past memory how to deal with a present problem, nothing more. It's our computer, our memory bank. But when we act as if our brain is all we have and the present loving moment doesn't exist, those old tapes become our reality and can harm us terribly. The only love we have then is in our brain, and that kind of love is just a definition, not a feeling. We think we love. We don't feel love. There's no power in that kind of love.

Old tapes are what hold us in negativity. We have to break this pattern. And only the *experience* of love is strong enough to do it. We must get in touch with our own essence which is love. That's where the power and energy is. If each of those two people had been in touch with their own essence strongly enough, he wouldn't have worried and she wouldn't have ached. But even if they were rank beginners, even a thimbleful of self love would have been enough to stop the old tapes and allowed them to deal lovingly with each other in the present moment.

So, we need to see that we *are* love. We are a part of God. But we are no big thing. We're nothing special. There's nothing to do. There's nothing for us to become, we already are. There's no work to be done, no effort to be put forth. We simply plunk down our body and rest for a while. God makes the potatoes grow, we just have to pick up the hoe and do our simple work. It's no big thing. God lets the change sink into us. We just have to pull the weeds once in a while. We have to recognize that all of our frantic activity isn't accomplishing anything, it's just getting in the way.

We don't need to talk to God, and God doesn't need to talk to us. We just have to open our hearts and let our essence flow. We have to give our brain a rest and let it become a simple tool, not our master.

Jackie and I have spent hours almost every day talking to each other for over thirty years now. We have never bored each other. She is the most fascinating woman I have ever known. But I think our most loving moments have come when we are just quiet together. Maybe she is holding a corral pole for me while I pound the nails. Or she is sitting across the room and we are both reading and we just glance at each other. Or I wake up in the night and have no covers and find her curled up in a ball near the foot of the bed. Or she looks out the kitchen window and sees my head sticking up above the steam of the hot tub. There is a feeling in those moments. It has nothing to do with our mind, the computer is turned off. But God, the power of that present moment. That's where love is. And the more of those the better. Accept those quiet moments and be grateful for them. The curse of love is trying to understand. Like Zorba the Greek said to the professor, "You think too much."

Chapter Four

OUR NEGATIVITY IS IN OUR MIND

Every so often we get out of our negative, cloudy frame of mind and see the clear, sunny sky of the spirit, life. We think, "Whoopee, I've got it made. I'm a new person, no more problems for me!" Then, the next thing we know we're right back in depression soup, full of negativity. What causes this? How can we better understand what's going on so we can take steps to protect ourself from this roller-coaster thinking?

An idea I've found helpful is to identify a part of myself as my mind. I then see that what I call mind has powerful advantages to me. It can store up all kinds of knowledge that helps me find my way around in the world and solve all kinds of problems. But the very way my mind works to solve those problems is the source of most of my troubles.

The mind works for me so well because it can be grooved. That's its nature. Forty-four years ago, when I was ten years old, I struggled to learn the multiplication tables. I finally learned the nines and I could remember what 9 × 7 was and what 9 × 8 was. In the forty-four years since then those grooves have been in my mind working for me. I was a very good student in school. What that meant was that my mind was more easily grooved than some others, and the grooves stayed put better than others. So the nature of the mind is to be grooved, and I have a mind that is a fine example of its nature.

Where I got into problems was that my mind took control of *all* the areas of my life. As long as my mind was solving arithmetic problems and telling me the way to the grocery store, its grooved nature worked great. But when my mind got into the spiritual level and took over my relationships with God and my fellow men (God made visible), I had all kinds of problems. My mind was grooved with my early childhood imaginings of God. He was the judge, the scorekeeper, the punisher. My mind stayed grooved like that.

So why should I turn my life over to such a God? That was God as I understood him then and he was awful, he was scary, and he was useless.

This whole picture would be pretty hopeless if my mind had complete control. It has a lot of control, but once in a while it finally gets beat down and tired and discouraged enough to let the voice of the spirit, or the higher mind, be heard.

The voice of the spirit, or the higher mind, is not grooved by nature; just the opposite. Its nature is to be free and to be continually able to change its position as new information is made available. So when my spirit heard the concept that I could have a different God than my awful childish one, it understood that and received the vision of a kind, loving God who was one with all and existed in all. But then the mind would get rested up and come roaring back demanding complete control.

When the spirit would try to be heard, the mind would snort something like, "Don't give me that God stuff. Remember when your grandmother was dying and you prayed to God she wouldn't die? What happened? Grandma died, didn't she?" So we would go back to mind, and the mind would make us dance like a monkey.

But as more and more hell and chaos came into our life, the mind gave up quicker for longer periods of time and let the spirit have its time. The spirit voice got stronger, it produced peace and order and harmony. It found that meditation was good. It found that concentration on the breathing could still the mind. And more and more, the one that is body-mind-spirit together began to question the mind's cries for supremacy and absolute rule and its insatiable hunger for more power, and it insisted that the reason the mind hadn't solved all our problems was because we had held back some power. If we would just give it all the power, then it would turn defeat into victory.

So that is the battle, back and forth between mind and higher mind. As I've watched this battle within myself, I'm finally able to make sense out of a lot of things I couldn't comprehend before. I'm finally getting smart enough to know how dumb I really was. I'm beginning to learn the things you learn after you know it all. As it says in the I Ching, the lower mind is right and wrong, the higher mind is no thing.

A while ago my wife put up a good sign for me on my bathroom mirror that says, "Don't seek truth, just stop having opinions."

No matter how clearly I see the spiritual, my mind comes roaring back. My mind shows its power by resisting meditation for the spirit. It says, "You don't have time. You don't need that." My mind tells me how smart I am. I've never heard anyone say their mind is bad. They will admit their ignorance about math or mechanical things, but they don't honestly say they are dumb about life. You can almost see the cunning of the mind as they sit in their mess. Why do we know our minds are so smart? Because our minds tell us we're smart.

My mind resists exercise for the body. Or it leaps into an excess of exercise, like when I started an exercise program of running after a heart attack. My stopwatch was in my hand and my chart with all my times was on the wall. That's what I was needing to get away from.

Slowly, I'm coming to the practice of a balance of the mind with the body-spirit. It's like the three horses in a troika, the three-horse Russian carriage. When the three horses of body-spirit-mind are in harmony, each pulls smoothly to the pace set by the middle horse, the spirit. When the mind acts up and starts jumping around seeking dominance, the harmony goes and movement stops.

Another control system of the mind when faced by truth is to laugh it off as just words. Pilate, when faced by Christ, fell back on scoffing, "Truth, what is truth?"

There is a story about a man who came to a teacher and asked, "Why should I say God's name? It has no power."

The teacher just looked at him and said, "You sure are a silly ass!" At this the man became very angry and stormed and yelled at the teacher. When he finally quieted down, the teacher said, "Look how much power one little word has. Think how much more power the name of God has."

We can use that power to still the mind. When we say God's name we are God because for that instant we are completely one with God.

Jackie was meditating one day and the words "heavy attitude" came to her in reference to herself, me, and others. My first thought was of myself before my heart attack where I was so full of what was right, I could discourse at length on any subject. I didn't go to my brother-in-law's wedding when he remarried because good religious people don't do things like that. Or, I remember telling Mary Ellen Olson and Bill Holbrook that we were going to build a bomb shelter. I'll never forget Mary Ellen's questioning attitude about what I was saying. It was like she felt a part of me was crazy.

The heart attack broke up that pattern and sent me looking for a better way for me. Many of my old attitudes were broken up, and I was more receptive to the people around me looking for new ways. I was even open enough to my eighteen-year-old students to ask them how they felt and to put my thinking out for them. I even asked them how they would be best taught. I was happy and excited at the ways our minds and hearts met.

There was some of the old there though. I was so insistent on using my one speech formula that one student, Joe Erickson, rebelled and really fought me on it. But even that I came to appreciate.

What I later saw in my own meditation was that I was like a little child with my pattern of stones laid out in the dirt believing in the magic of the pattern. My heart attack broke up the pattern. But instead of staying away from patterns, I gradually went back to having a new pattern. So now there's a large part of me that just can't wait until someone opens up and tells me their problem so I can fix it. So much of the wonder and questioning of the beginner's mind is gone, and my expert's mind sees so few possibilities.

I saw in meditation that my big problem was fear of the unknown and a lack of trust in God. I went on a new quest for certainty and supported my rightness with my success and the fact that so many of a certain kind of people wanted to be around me. But I knew that was hollow.

I see the reflection of this in my increasing success in relationships with people. The reason I feel so good on hunting trips is that it keeps me away from my crap. We just enjoy each other. Same at the two stores downtown where I stop in a lot, the Powderhorn Sporting Goods store and Owenhouse Hardware. The people in those stores and I just like each other.

The first book I wrote happened because I loved nurses and appreciated what they had done for me rather than because I knew all the things nurses were doing wrong and would be good at fixing them.

I guess it adds up to what my kids have been telling me—"lighten up, Dad," lighten up in body and spirit. As Ray Hunt says, "Go whistling and grinning through the day." I need to spend more time waiting for the good things God has for me in the day rather than waiting for something to fix.

Another characteristic of the mind is negativity. Nothing is ever good enough for the mind. We need the mind to evaluate and judge things. That's its function. When the mind is telling us that these oranges are a better buy than those oranges, this bid on a job is better than that bid, that's the mind at its best. But the mind doesn't stop there. It goes off into all areas and judges. So the mind gets into spiritual areas and judges people, it judges religions, it even judges God. The result is a constant negativity. Nothing is ever right. Nothing is ever good enough and the load of negativity in us builds up and up.

A thief came to a Zen master's house with a sword and said, "Give me your money." The Zen master said, "It is over there. Go help yourself." The thief went over and started taking the money. The Zen master then said, "By the way, I have to pay my taxes next week. Leave me enough to pay my taxes." The thief left enough money for the taxes. As the thief was going out the door the Zen master said, "When someone gives you a gift you thank him for it." So the thief said, "Thank you."

Some weeks later the thief was caught robbing someone else. He confessed to robbing the Zen master also so the Zen master was required to come to court to testify against the thief. The Zen master testified, "That man did not steal any money from me. I gave him the money and he thanked me for it."

The thief served his prison term. When it was over he came to the Zen master to begin the study of Zen. That is a story about what it means to live without negativity.

Another Zen master lived high on a mountainside in a very lonely spot. He was a very poor man. He returned home one night and found a robber ransacking his humble home. The robber could find nothing of value. The Zen master said, "Here, take my cloak so you won't have to go home empty-handed." The robber took the cloak and left.

The old Zen master then went outside his hut and sat down on his bench to look at the beautiful moon. "The moon is so beautiful," he thought. "It's too bad I couldn't have gotten it for the robber and given it to him."

That's also what it means to live without negativity.

A young unmarried girl got pregnant by a young village boy. Her parents found out that she was pregnant and forced her to say who the father was. The girl was terrified and so she lied. "The Zen master is the father of my child," she said.

After the child was born the girl's parents took the child to the Zen master and said, "Here is your child. Our daughter told us you are the father. We are poor people and cannot afford this child, you take it." The Zen master looked at the child and said, "Is that so?" He took the child into his home to love and to raise.

Some years later the girl could no longer live with her lie and she confessed to her parents. The parents were horrified. They went to the Zen master and said, "Our daughter has confessed her lie. Give us the child. We will love and raise the child." The Zen master said, "Is that so?" and gave the child to them.

That's another story about living without negativity. This is what you and I need to learn. We need to see that all negativity comes out of us, out of our mind. All negativity comes out of a lack of understanding of God, of love.

There have been a few times in my life when I have been able to experience a freedom from negativity and it is a beautiful experience.

One time a wealthy gentleman called me. He had read my first book, *I Ain't Much Baby—But I'm All I've Got*. He wanted me to come to his city and "save" a few of his friends. He threw a few names around, names of famous people who were his friends. He said they needed me. One of those names was a famous sports idol of mine. My ego liked the idea, but I was able to say, "I'm sorry but I don't feel that I need to come to your city to save anybody. I don't think they need me." Then this man said, "Well then, can I fly to Bozeman and have a cup of coffee with you?" That was a nice expensive thing to do. I was properly impressed with his power by now. But I was still able to handle what was happening and I said, "Yes."

He flew to Bozeman. He was really a nice guy. Jackie and I went out to dinner with him. We arrived in Jackie's old Chevrolet. The dinner was nice and we really liked this guy. But his world was not our world. Halfway through dinner he told us he was stopping in Bozeman on his way to Europe to the Porsche factory to pick up an expensive turbo Porsche he had bought. Then he was going to northern Africa to check on some oil properties. He was a real, genuine jet-setter.

Now don't get me wrong. He didn't say things to put us down. That was him, that was his life-style. He saw himself as no different than us. As I said, Jackie and I really liked him and saw that he was a nice, gentle person.

As we left the restaurant and were walking to our car we saw that our car wasn't there. Jackie and I couldn't believe it. We thought maybe we'd forgotten where we'd parked it. We looked around the parking lot, but our car wasn't there. There was finally only one conclusion, someone had stolen our car. So I said, "Well, our car's been stolen. I'll call Dave Sullivan and he'll take us home." I called Dave and he said he'd come and get us. So we turned and thanked the gentleman for the evening and for coming to Bozeman.

He couldn't stand it anymore. "My God, Jess," he yelled, "you act like your car is stolen every day. My God, aren't you going to call the police? Aren't you going to do something?" His distress was obvious.

I laughed and said, "It's all right. Somebody probably just borrowed it."

That left our wealthy friend, who had just spent more money than our car was worth to fly to Bozeman, as frustrated as hell because I wasn't as excited as he was.

The next day the police called. A drunk had come out of the restaurant, gotten into our car and driven it to Livingston before he realized it wasn't his car. I was so glad that I hadn't gotten all steamed up about my stolen car and angry at whoever had stolen it.

Another time, not too long ago, I had a hat I really loved. It had silver conchos on it, a real rhinestone cowboy's hat. I was at a meeting and when I came out after the meeting my hat was gone. "Well," I thought, "somebody needed my hat worse than I did." So I went downtown and bought a new hat, and I decided to make a new hatband for myself. I bought some turquoise from my friend Dave Petty and made myself a new hatband. After a while Dave came to Bozeman with a woman's silver concho belt. I added that as a second hatband along with the turquoise one, and it looked gorgeous. Then I realized why somebody stole my hat. It was because I needed this beautiful new hatband.

In those two instances it was a good thing to see myself approach them in a non-negative way. I don't mean to say I manage that that often. Hell, if you take a crust off my plate I'll pound you.

There are other times I have a lot of negativity and it shows. When Jackie and I were in Arizona, I was going to play golf. Jackie came with me to drive the cart and just be with me. I went to hit some practice balls and Jackie went into the clubhouse to pay for my nine holes and rent a golf cart. When she came out she said, "How much does it cost to play golf here?" I said, "Three dollars." I looked at the receipt and the guy had punched three dollars twice. So while Jackie went to get the cart I went in to find out what happened. I thought maybe the guy had charged me for eighteen holes. The guy said, "No. Your wife said that the two of you were going to play." And then he said something about non-players not understanding the ways of golf, and I nice and passively agreed with him that my wife didn't understand about golf. Well, Jackie had come up behind me and heard me. I felt ashamed or afraid she'd blow up and I got real quiet and negative toward her right away.

Jackie didn't say anything and we went out and got into the cart and she started to drive to the tee. Well, to get to the tee Jackie had to drive down a hill and make a sharp right turn, and it was right in front of the clubhouse. She didn't make the turn fast enough, and the cart went up on the back of the tee and then down to the path. Over the loudspeaker the guy yells, "Lady, we don't drive on the tees. Stay twenty feet away from the tees at all times or I'll have to ask you to leave the golf course."

I knew Jackie was upset and embarrassed and so was I, but I

didn't say anything. I just got out of the cart and teed off. I got back in the cart and Jackie started driving and I knew she was beside herself, but I was being negative toward her by then so I was silent.

We drove down the fairway in silence and finally Jackie said, "What did that guy say to you in the clubhouse?" "He told me you said you wanted to pay for the two of us to play golf," I answered. Jackie looked at me, steaming, "Why would I say that? I don't play golf. What did you say?" "Well, I didn't know what was going on, I didn't know what you'd said." Nice and passive and negative you see.

"I want to go back and kill that guy and you too," Jackie said. "You treat me like you think I'm a liar, like you think I asked for two golf tickets, like you don't give a damn that he mortified me over that loudspeaker. Can't you just say that the guy's a jerk and that you know I didn't ask for two tickets and that he was wrong to yell at me on the loudspeaker?" And my wife started to cry. And she cried on that golf course for quite a ways. Finally, I gave her a little support, but she'd had to pull it from me.

In retrospect what I should have said was, "Hey, honey, you are very clear when you say things and I believe you. That guy was a jerk to yell over the loudspeaker." But it was my negativity toward Jackie showing in my actions.

The very things I love about Jackie, the things I married her for also cause us the most pain in our relationship. She's a very straightforward, honest, up-front lady. You always know where you're at with her. She's outgoing and energetic and kind and good-hearted. Crabby sometimes, like in the morning, but most of the time she's pretty easy to get along with. She's the only woman in the world who I have always found interesting, and she's gorgeous! Now with all of those attributes, why would I be negative?

I'm Norwegian you see. I always said that I wouldn't know a feeling if I met one on the street. I've always been terrified of emotionality at the same time that I'm fascinated by it. And I always run from emotionality if I even suspect it might be around. I try to control it and keep it away. So when I get into a situation where there is the potential for deep feelings being displayed in public, or even at home, most of the time I run. Have I ever seen Jackie blow up in public and scream and yell and curse at someone? No. She's never done that. Sometimes when we're traveling and we're tired and our luggage is lost or our hotel reservations are fouled up, she's a lot more forceful than I want her to be, and then I tell her through gritted teeth to shut up and let me handle it. But my wife is not a woman who has ever made an ass of herself or me. So why? Where does this fear and negativity come from?

The negativity comes from me. I choose it. I've chosen it for more years than I've known Jackie. By now I've worn negativity grooves deep into my brain. It's become a habit that's hurting me and my relationship with my wife. I know I'd better do something about it or else face why I won't do anything about it.

My wife and I have over thirty years of negative things stored up against each other. Most couples only have to go together a few weeks and the stockpile has begun, their computer bank of negative tapes. Jackie has these too. She was playing negative tapes in that incident too. She was playing all the times I'd done the same thing to her in her head or she would have been able to laugh and say, "Listen to that silly ass over the loudspeaker, Jess. Isn't he being stupid?" But she couldn't do that. Negativity had her too.

Jackie won't mind my telling you that her biggest negativity is toward men in that golf pro's position who are so afraid of women and so afraid of being wrong that they lie to protect themselves. She's downright contemptuous of them. She cannot abide men who will not act like men. Afterward she recognized that I knew this about her and that I had a right to be afraid that maybe this would be the day that she might decide to tell this representative of irresponsible manhood just how she viewed him and every other man like him! I had to recognize that she's never ever done this in public, so my fear was stupid and foolish. And finally we could laugh together about the whole incident.

What happens when we play old tapes is that we don't have the direct experience of reality. We use old tapes to avoid the direct experience of reality. We use them to keep us locked into our negativity. That's familiar ground. We can handle that. We've lived and survived that way for years. It's all we know. There's no risk in continuing to play those old tapes, it's painful but it's territory we know. That's our world as we see it.

The day comes for most of us though when the pain and isolation caused by our negativity is too much for us. We finally cry out, "God. Is this all there is?" That's called a crisis. In crisis a lot of times, we do some still greater negative things, like we run away, we have nervous breakdowns, we divorce, we get drunk, or sometimes even try to take our lives. All those things are still more negativity heaped on all the rest of our negativity, but we're so locked into it that we don't know what else to do.

Negativity is a very expensive habit. It's cost us our happiness, our peace of mind. I've known men who have quit fifty-thousand-dollar-a-year jobs, just like that, because they didn't like the way their boss parted his hair. They used old tapes of negativity to build them to a pitch where a little thing like the boss's hair caused them to quit a decent job. Then they used those old tapes and old saws like, "The straw that broke the camel's back," to justify what they did. They use their old tapes to avoid the direct experience of the reality, and the next thing they know they're out on the street with no job, and not much chance of another.

What do old tapes do? They feed our egos. One thing we had better understand about our ego—our ego can never be wrong. Our ego will take anything and twist it any way it can to convince us that it is right. Our ego speaks to us through our mind. Our ego is what made our mind our master instead of our servant. Our ego is that part of us that tells us we have to "be somebody."

We need our ego. Don't get me wrong. With no ego strength we'd all be helpless. We need ego to have the strength to look inside ourselves and to find the essence of ourselves, which is love. What we don't need is the ego that is nothing but self-will run riot. What we don't need is the ego that keeps us like little babies having temper tantrums. That kind of ego is killing us. There's no balance in the ego that keeps us locked into negativity in order to avoid the direct experience of reality.

A nice, proper ego tells me that I'm a nice little fellow and that most people like me quite a bit and that the world is a pretty good place to live in and that I'm not going to starve to death today and that I'm worthy of good things happening in my life. And that's it. I'm not a giant, but I'm not a dwarf either. I'm just me. No big beans, and that's all right. That's what our ego is supposed to tell us. But our egos go way past that into negativity.

Can you see the possibilities for yourself if you could put down your negativity? Can you see what life could be like for you if you changed your mind about yourself? Could you see what life could be like if you began to live each day in the present moment with the direct experience of reality?

I can hear you. "Jess doesn't know what it's like for me. He doesn't live with the drunken bum I do." I ask you, "Where is that drunken man right this minute? Is he doing something right now that is stopping you from calling a friend to tell that friend you love her? Is that drunken bum beating you right now so that you can't look out the window and marvel at the sun or the rain or the grass or the snow? Is that drunken bum stopping you from making the kids a cup of hot cocoa with a marshmallow in it—and drinking a cup yourself? If he is, then you'd better go to Al-Anon or go and get some professional help because you're as sick as he is." I'm sorry, but that's how I see it.

"Jess doesn't know what it's like for me though. My wife is a total bitch, and right now she's out playing and I'm working my butt off." That's interesting. Is she such a bitch that you don't have any friends who love you? Is she stopping you from enjoying this minute with a friend or one of your kids? Is she spending you into the poorhouse? Is she playing around with another guy and you're just letting it happen? If that's true, you'd better go to Emotions Anonymous or get some professional help. You're as sick as she is.

These are just imaginary projections about how readers might react. But in those reactions you can see how the ego demands to be right. Self-righteous is another way of saying it. Boy, is self-righteousness cold soup! I've never seen that attitude solve a problem or bring love into anyone's life.

Right now I could join a country club in Arizona for ten thousand dollars and two thousand a year in dues. That's a lot of money! But what kind of money have we paid to stay in our negativity? What price, just in money alone, has our ego demanded? Most of us manage to lose a thousand dollars, two or three times a year through extravagance, stupidity, or refusing money that we deserve by saying to ourselves, "No, it must belong to someone else, I don't deserve riches." We blow money, we lose it, we neglect it, we are blind in our purchases. We're soft touches for giving money where it'll make us look big. I'd guess that, for many of us, an expensive country club is a much cheaper deal than our negative club. When you quit the country club you can sell your membership and get your ten thousand back. No one gets back the money they lose to negativity and ego problems.

In my lifetime I've paid dues ten times what that country club would cost me because of my negativity toward money. I have gone to a lot of trouble to push away the riches of the world that I said I wanted. It's like the world said to me, "Here, Jess, take it, it's free." And I pushed it away at the same time I said I wanted it. That's the direct experience of a reality of mine. I did that to myself.

One time I was giving a retreat for some priests in a western province of Canada. I drove my car to Great Falls, Montana, and flew up from there. Flying back to Great Falls I decided to try to have as much of the direct experience of reality as I could —to be here in the moment.

So, I landed and got out my car keys and walked to my car. The battery was dead because I'd left my lights on for those three days. I wanted to get negative. "Isn't it dumb how I left my lights on!" and stuff like that. But I didn't let it happen. I started looking around for whoever God or love was going to send to me to help solve my problem.

Two men were walking across the parking lot. I went over and told them my problem and asked if they could help. One guy said, "That's no problem. Here's the keys to my car. It's over there. Drive my car over to yours and jump the battery. When you get through, just park my car and leave the keys on the seat."

I said, "Thank you," and did just that. All the time I'm shaking my head saying, "Wow!" That was a beautiful, positive direct experience of reality. I thought about my first reaction. For a second I'd thought, "Damn. I'm ten miles from town. I'll have to call a wrecker, and it will cost me a lot of money." But that wasn't what happened. I was lucky with my first direct experience of reality. I jumped my battery and left a ten dollar bill on the seat of the guy's car.

So then I got in my car and started driving down the road

watching the scenery. I wanted to experience being in my car and seeing what was going on in the moment. I've driven that road many times, but I've never seen the scenery. Pretty soon I realized that I'd driven quite a ways again and I still hadn't seen anything. My mind was in last week somewhere. So I started looking at the scenery again. I said to myself, "I'm going to be in this car right now." This kept happening and happening. Each time I would get my mind out of last week or next month or wherever it was and back into now. One time I found my mind had drifted a long ways away. When I finally came to I realized that my arms were so tense on the steering wheel that they ached. There was no need for that. I've got power steering in my car. I relaxed my arms and drove with just my fingertips, and had to smile. I saw again how hard it was to have the direct experience of reality.

The best way I can explain how to have the direct experience of reality is that we come to live in a meditative way all day long. We quit identifying ourselves with our bodies or our minds. We become our own observers. We step away from what we have always assumed was us and watch ourselves from our own essence, from love. We realize we're not who we thought we were. We realize we're all wrapped up in being the body, in being the mind, in being hurt and antagonized. We step into our essence and detach from all that nonsense, and then we're not all caught up in our own soap opera. Ram Dass calls our soap opera our "mellow-drama." Our mellow-drama is not who we are, it's who we're choosing to be at that moment. It's nonsense, and it helps us to see that we've got to stop it because it's hurting us.

When my battery was dead, if I'd thrown myself to the ground and beat my fists against the ground until they bled, what good would it have done? Don't laugh. I've done things that childish. That would have been a real "mellow-drama," I'll tell you. But as we say, instead I "mellowed-out," I stepped back.

Jackie's friend, the Idiot of Bernbach, admits openly that he's a very angry man. But you'd never know it. He's one of the sweetest, most gentle, laughing, loving human beings you'll ever meet. Jackie's convinced she's met St. Francis living today, but Jackie gets a little carried away sometimes. What did this man do for himself that took him away from being a very angry man?

He chose to step back from that anger, to realize that wasn't him. He chose to walk with his God-self, his essence, to walk in love instead. If he'd stayed with his mellow-drama, he couldn't have been Jackie's teacher, she couldn't have seen his essence. And the power of his essence changed my wife's life, just like the power of Muktananda's essence helped to change mine.

Does the fact that some people live in their essence mean that suddenly they are placid saints walking around dull and boring? No. They still even get angry! But they are angry just in the moment at just what has happened in that moment without bringing in a lot of nonsense remembered from the past or feared in the future. And the anger is a special kind of anger where they are only part angry. Another quiet part of themselves is watching themselves be angry. So it's a very different kind of anger for them and the people around them. These people laugh a lot more, too. They see the joy of the many beautiful, funny, touching things that happen in their day.

What I've seen with the lost car story and the hat story is that they were direct experiences of reality, and because they were I was able to be in the next moment after that and be really there instead of licking my wounds and slipping into negativity. Because I was able to do that I was able to have the benefit of continuing on with the relationship I was in at the moment instead of slipping off into some other place and some other time in my mind.

Two monks were walking down a muddy street through a small village. They saw a young woman in a beautiful kimono on one side of the street who was obviously wondering how she could cross over to the other side. One of the two monks went over, picked her up and carried her across the street.

They walked on and the second monk didn't say anything. Finally that evening he could stand it no longer. "About that beautiful woman," he said, "we monks aren't supposed to go near beautiful women, say nothing of carrying them across a street!"

The second monk said, "Are you still carrying her? I put her down in the market place this morning."

Most of us spend a lot of time carrying the past around with us. Are you still carrying those old resentments, that bitterness, that envy, that self-pity, that jealousy, that agony, that fear, that inadequacy, that stupidity, that sense of inferiority, that sense that you're separate from God? Are you still carrying that? You don't have to. You can put it all down right now in a nice little pile on the floor there in front of you and walk away and leave it all there. Every bit of it. Nobody put it in you or on you. You chose to pick it up and carry it all of this time, and you can choose to leave it now and forevermore. You had a choice, and you gradually and continuously chose that negativity. And even if some of that was part of your human condition, you long ago had the choice to put various pieces of it down and you chose not to. You said, "I'm going to hang on to this. I'm going to keep carrying it." But you have a new choice right now. You can choose to put it down, let it go.

One of the most powerful stories I've heard recently is about a woman who finally decided, under a certain tough set of circumstances, to leave a marriage of many years. She walked through the home she had helped to create over a period of thirty years and realized that there was nothing there she wanted or needed. She left thirty years of her life behind and walked out of that house with nothing in her hands.

You see, when we decide that we will be free, there is nothing in the world that will stop us. There is nothing that we need, no old baggage to carry along. We just let go and walk away. When we decide to divorce our negativity then we will do it. If we don't do it, then we must face that. What need of ours is being served by our negativity? What is our negativity doing for us that we hang on to it so tightly? What purpose does it serve?

Some of us face the fact that our negativity is an old familiar friend and that we don't know how to live without it. We want it. That too is a choice some of us could make. But it is a choice made out of fear of the unknown. A fear of risk. It is the old saying, "'Who was it, prisoner, who forged your chains so carefully?' 'It was I,' said the prisoner, 'who forged my chains so carefully.'"

We are like prisoners in a cell with three walls. We stand and beat our fists on the walls and scream, "Let me out." Yet we will not turn and see that there is no fourth wall, that we can walk right out of our cell.

We're like the man in the story my friend Walther Lechler tells.

A man builds a home. Then he builds a high wall around his

home. Inside those walls he has gardens and a cow and some chickens and he grows vegetables and he has a reasonable world built for himself. But sometimes he gets lonely, so he climbs to the top floor of his home and gazes out across the wall. In the distance he sees vast meadows and mountains and lakes, and great beauty. In the meadows he sees cattle grazing and cowboys riding horses, tending to the cattle. Some nights he sees the cowboys gathering around a campfire eating. If the wind blows right, sometimes he can hear them singing and laughing. The man feels lonely and wishes he could be with them. But he never goes outside his walls. He is comfortable after a fashion, and he doesn't want to take the risk.

Then one day a terrible wind comes that blows down the man's house and destroys his garden and tears down his wall. He is forced to go out into the world beyond.

He walks and walks and sees the cowboys. They are kind to him and offer him food and shelter. Finally, the man asks the cowboys who all of this beautiful land belongs to. The cowboys say a man who lives over there in a house with a high wall owns it. They say to the man how strange it is that the man that owns this land never comes and enjoys it. They do all the work and enjoy the land, but the man never comes. The man knows they are speaking of him, he is the owner of this land.

Then the man becomes really fearful, because now he knows he must make a choice. Either he stays out here in his land and possesses it, or else he goes back and rebuilds his house and wall. This is crisis. This is the point most of us face right now. Shall we take the risk and put our negativity down, or shall we stay with the safety of the known, limited and miserable as it is?

Most of us live a life that is choked off because of fences and walls we have created that have no reason. We say, "But I've been hurt." No! We haven't been hurt. Our ego was bruised a little, but we created this artificial ego and it deserves to be hurt.

We have created egos that are like balloons. We have surrounded ourselves with fifty big, blown-up balloons. We have them tied all over us, and we want to be able to walk downtown without anyone ever touching our balloons or without a cigarette ever brushing us and blowing up one of our balloons. If one of our balloons get touched or blown up, we are destroyed. "Oh woe is me, life has treated me badly. My bright blue balloon got punctured by a man who walked by me in a crowd with a pin sticking out of his pocket. I must take my forty-nine balloons home and stay in my house with them or they'll get broken too. My God! I can't even go downtown with my forty-nine balloons without one of them getting broken."

One of my negativities is the belief that I'm inferior and people don't like me. That shows itself very clearly at times; most notably in a dream I had the other night. I dreamed that I was back at the University of Minnesota and I was having a miserable time with my job. (This part of the dream is pretty factual. I don't think I ever got along well on any job I ever had. That's why I always ended up working for myself or by myself). In the dream I was a professor, and I was miserable and alone walking down the halls of the Journalism School. I came walking by the Dean's office and he was on the phone. I stopped and listened in. He was working on a project in consumer marketing with someone, and that was my field. He hadn't told me about it or included me in any way. I felt hurt and inadequate and out of it. No one wanted to be my friend, and it was awful.

So, in my dream I went home feeling this way and walked into the house all hurt and negative and there was Jackie just steaming. She had gone over to the psychology department, which was my other logical department, and she had lined up a research project with a fine psychologist there named Dr. Del-Gado. She had gotten me a $2,500 grant and a chance to work with him. She told me that she had lined this up and that he really wanted to work with me. I sensed that what she was really saying was, "You whimpering oaf, quit feeling sorry for yourself and get your butt in gear and get out of that cry-baby attitude of yours."

This was my dream, and it took me until ten in the morning to muster enough guts to tell Jackie what I had dreamed. It doesn't take anyone deep in Freudian analysis to understand the significance of that dream, I'll tell you.

Our costumes are often a part of our negativity, also. We dress up or down in order to give a picture of ourselves to the world. Because I feel inferior I have to have the right costume on. Right? I wanted to go to a horse sale down in Phoenix, so I put on my cowboy costume. I had on Levi's and a western shirt and my summer cowboy hat, which is a straw hat with a lot of silver conchos on it. And I had on my cowboy belt buckle, which was all gold and silver. So not only did I have the appropriate costume on when I went to the horse sale, but I looked semi-splendid! I walked into the horse sale, and here's a bunch of cowboys all seeing my splendid outfit and nobody says a word. I didn't even get a "howdy."

A week later, I was driving down the road in a pair of shorts and a golf shirt and sandals, and I remembered that there was a horse sale that day. I wanted to go but I didn't have my costume on. I realized I didn't have time to go home and dress cowboy so everyone would know that I belonged there. I had to decide, do I go to the horse sale dressed like this or forget it? I thought, "What the hell! Just go to the sale." And I went.

So I went over there and plunked myself down next to an old cowboy, and right away he starts talking to me.

Afterward I asked myself why did he respond to me right away this time and no one spoke to me last time? I realized it was simple. A guy in shorts and sandals looks like he just wandered in off the street. He isn't going to intimidate a cowboy at a horse sale. He doesn't look like a big horse buyer from Texas.

It's like you gals, you're at a party in your nice dress and you're comfortable until the one gal in the crowd with a real expensive designer original dress comes over and sits down beside you. What do you say to her? What do you have in common with her? You both have dresses on, but you know and she knows that hers cost a thousand dollars more than yours. You feel intimidated and shy all of a sudden, don't you? Well, I say that's what my shiny splendor did to the cowboys at the first horse sale. I'd done a number on those guys at that sale, the "Electric Horseman."

We all have our areas where we do feel secure. We're not all 100 percent negative. I used to have an old jeep, "the Green Bean." I drove that wreck everywhere. Even driving on paved streets she rattled your teeth. Conversation was impossible in her, she was so noisy. One day my friend Jerry Sullivan said, "Boy, Jess. You've sure got to be secure with yourself to drive a wreck like this." I was secure—in that area.

Our minds keep us locked in negativity. Our mind keeps saying, "I can do it for you." And every failure our mind hands us, it just tells us, "Give me one more chance, I know I can do it."

We condemn alcoholics because they won't give up alcohol, but we cling to our negativity with equal fierceness.

I always remember a story told by Father Martin. He's the priest who goes around the world talking to recovering alcoholics and the like. He's famous in those circles for his "Chalk Talk." He tells about how one night he realized that an alcoholic is just like a prize fighter who walks into a ring every night to get his brains knocked out. He does this night after night after night. And he is carried out of the ring only to come back the next night. Finally, one night as he is just barely crawling into the ring, he hears a voice say, "Don't go in the ring." That's it! We don't need to go into the ring and fight alcoholism or negativity. We just put it down, let it be.

Our answers are so childishly simple we miss them. This is where our mind hurts us. The mind will never recognize its own stupidity. The mind takes us down and down until finally our soul screams out in agony, "I give up. I've had enough." Our mind won't see that we've had enough. We have to suffer enough to finally pierce our soul. And then our soul says, "No more, no more." Then we get the first glimpse that what we have been seeking out there is right inside of us. We hear our soul's voice and realize it is what we have been seeking all this time.

There is a simple test we can use to see how we're doing with our negativity. Our negativities are the holes that let our energy run out. The more we get rid of our negativities of anger, jealousy, resentment, and envy, the more energy we have left at the end of the day. When we're rid of negativity we have as much energy left at the end of the day as we started out with in the morning. I used to sink into my easy chair after supper and I literally couldn't get back out. Now I can sit in my easy chair and read the paper, then get up easily and do something else.

The one sure powerful tool I know of to help us get rid of negativity is to be a "confessed" person. None of us should have anything in our mind or heart that we have not shared with another human being.

If we say to ourselves, "I can't tell this to anyone," we are doubting love. We are negative about our self worth. We do not believe that God or our neighbor could love us enough. We are using that to stay in negativity. I don't care if you had sex with your own mother or father. It's no big thing if you don't cling to it. Let it go. Put it down. Walk away from negativity. It's killing you.

Now—for those of you who might be willing to become confessed persons, please pick who you confess to very carefully. If you have been sleeping with the man up the street, I don't think that it is wise to tell your husband or his wife or even a neighbor about this. Be careful and be discreet so that you don't wind up and confess and get blown away by a very negative reaction. If you do, be aware that you picked that person and ask yourself if this is just another way to set up a defeat for yourself. If you have a biggy you have carried around most of your life and you want to get rid of it, then I suggest going to a minister, a priest, or a trusted counselor.

The various twelve-step programs have people who specialize in doing this work. They call them fifth-step counselors. If you call any AA or EA office, they will give you the name of someone who has a lot of practice at listening to people just like you. Again I say, let go of your negativity. Put it down. Leave it and walk away. You don't need it anymore. Good Luck.

Chapter Five

ATTACHMENTS TO OUR OLD THINGS
AND OLD IDEAS

Another way to look at the way we are limited by our overconcentration on our mind is to consider our attachments.

Because of the grooved nature of our minds, we get in certain ways of thinking. As those set patterns of thinking go on and on, we identify with those patterns, we see ourselves as them. Some people feel so deeply about their political party, they are so attached to it, that it's hard for them to conceive of themselves as the same person if they were a member of the other party.

Another way we become attached is to things and ideas that act as a shell to hide our imagined inferiority. We can be attached to having fine clothes or fine cars or fine houses or fine jobs in an attempt to hide our sense of being second-rate. This comes from our mind constantly comparing and evaluating in areas where comparison and evaluation are inappropriate. You can compare two pitches in baseball and call one a ball, the other a strike. But you can't compare two people and call one good and the other one bad. Yet our mind is constantly comparing ourself to others, usually to our disadvantage. Our mind must seek the inferior in order to justify itself, to prove it's better. In our finite limited world, our mind justifies itself by discrimination and comparison.

Our deep attachments to dogs and cats come partly because none of us can feel inferior to an animal. We all talk about our inferiority complex, we're attached to that idea, without recognizing that our minds are inferior to God's, so why call it a complex? It's like this friend of mine who was so attached to the idea that he had an inferiority complex. We looked into it and found out that he really was inferior. What a relief! He didn't have to have a complex.

That's the lesson for all of us. We are all inferior. When we understand that then we don't have a problem. We don't have to be superior. We can let go of a lot of attachments that way. It's only our mind that creates that idea.

The attachments that are easiest to see are the ones that are material. The need to feel superior creates a lot of our material attachments. I'm so aware of that. If all of my clothes and cars and guns didn't have just the right label on them, I'd feel inferior. If I had a superior label on my clothes, I could feel good. Nowadays we're wearing those labels on the outside, too, so we can all compare. With a superior label on my clothes I could feel good because I had something I thought was superior covering up my unacceptable inferior interior. A man won't marry a woman who's smarter than him. He won't marry a woman who's taller than he is, or older either.

There's also spiritual materialism. We become attached to our way as the only way. Within our own denominations we even look at each other in church and mentally remark that we are saying our prayers with more feeling than somebody else, or that our children are going to church and their children aren't. Or the extreme, "I'm saved. You aren't." This attitude exists in meditation, too. "I had a better meditation today than I had last week." Or, "I meditate better than him." Or, "He meditates better than me."

All of this is of the mind, not the spirit. The spirit doesn't compare. It doesn't make these harmful discriminations. The spirit doesn't need attachments. Very early in life we make a series of choices about our different strategies in dealing with the world, and these are the beginnings of our attachments.

As a young boy in Bricelyn, Minnesota, I chose to decide that I lived on the wrong side of the tracks in the social scheme of things. Choosing that understanding left me two choices about handling my life. I could have said to myself, "Hey that's dumb. I'm going to smile and be nice and speak to whoever I want to and play with everyone, and to heck with this artificial stuff." Or I could say, "Boy, there must be something wrong with me. I'll withdraw and feel sorry for myself, and when I get big enough

I'll show them. I'll be the best in school and get rich and drive a fancy car, and then I'll feel better."

The latter is what I did. I began to gear myself for conspicuous success. My life became a constant seeking for power. Some of these things were very good—it wasn't all bad—but I became attached to material things to show the world my power. And I became grooved in that way. I wanted the best for myself, and I had to have it at all costs. I became tremendously attached to labels. But my biggest attachment was to the idea that things or places or people, something outside myself, could make me feel good. That's the same as an alcoholic thinking that alcohol will make him feel better, or a heroin addict thinking that the next fix is doing something for him.

I feel deeply about Bozeman in an honest way. I love the mountains and the scenery and the hunting and fishing and horseback riding and skiing, and the creativity I enjoy here. The attachment side of me felt that I needed Bozeman in order to feel good and function well. Even deeper, I believed I needed Bozeman to survive. In my earlier days I got to the place, in attachment, where most of the things I had, the pattern of life I had, the place where I lived, became overwhelmingly important to me to show me that I was all right. I also got to the place where these outward things were about the only satisfactions I had.

The power of attachments is that we come to believe we literally can't survive without them. We can't throw anything away, we can't move, we are no longer free.

In order to live—"I Walk Most Safely When I Don't Know Where I Go"—our attachments have got to go. We need to give up attachments before we can have a rebirth of any kind. We cannot change our thinking, our destructive attitudes, or any of our neuroses until we are willing to change our way of looking at the world.

When we are attached we are trapped just like the monkey. There was a banana in the cage. He reached through the bars of the cage for the banana. When he got the banana in his hands, he couldn't get his hand back out of the cage. So he was a prisoner.

The same way with attachments. If I hang on I'm caught in

the trap just like the monkey. I need to put down the things in my life before my hands can be free, and before my hands can be empty and open to receive the next new thing God has ready for me. No matter how fast I receive or how good what I receive is, I need to be always ready to put it all down and reach out again, with empty hands, so I can receive the next good thing God has for me.

A first step in this is to give up our need for the inferior. In my third book, *I Ain't Well—But I Sure Am Better*, I began to see this when I told of realizing that I couldn't have a friend unless I felt superior to them. When I first realized this it told me plenty about myself. I couldn't feel good unless I could look down on my friends! Some friend I was. I then realized that I needed to go to good, strong people for friendships. In a sense, I at first had to seek what I saw as the superior in order to begin this journey toward putting down my attachment to feeling inferior.

Jackie was working on her book *I Exist, I Need, I'm Entitled* with Walther Lechler in his Psychosomatische Klinic in Bad Herrenalb, West Germany. While there she had the opportunity to observe a lot of people. She noticed one woman doctor at the clinic in particular, and she went to Walther and said, "What is it with that woman? She only comes to life when she is around sick people." Walther said, "You noticed that did you? She needs sick people in order to feel well."

When Jackie told me about this I was struck with how that story was applicable in almost all of our lives. We all seek that which makes us feel good. If we have the strength to take an honest look at that which we seek, we will have a chance to learn so much about ourselves. Our attachments help us see who we think we are.

About five years ago I began to study Alpha Awareness with Wally Minto. He was so struck by this and said to me, "Jess, you're the first person with any prominence who is willing to listen to me instead of trying to teach me." That willingness to be taught took me to Baba Muktananda. I could not begin to seek what I saw as superior until I began to believe that it was all right to be inferior. It's all right. God is big, I am little. That's good. I am inferior to God, and as such I am inferior and it's no big thing. Everyone and everything is inferior to God. That's beautiful; that's us. That's no complex. But it is a place to start.

I know that while in a sense I am inferior to God, in a larger sense, I'm not. God's in me and I'm in God, so there can be no inferior. But I see that our finite, limited minds need a place to start. And they are so used to comparing that there may be some help in starting with the idea that God is big and I am little.

We can't drop our ego until we're willing to feel inferior. Look at how much simpler the world is when I realize that I'm just a little guy from the boonies of Bozeman. I've written some books and I've got a Ph.D., but it's no big thing. I don't need those books or that degree to tell me who I am. I'm nothing special. Just a little guy doing his work and laughing and scratching along the way.

When I see that I'm just a little guy, when I'm not attached to being superior because I feel inferior, it simplifies my day so much for me. Then when some policeman stops my car and says, "Hey, you idiot, didn't you see that red light? I don't need to defend myself and try to make him see that I'm a real smart guy. I can say, "No, officer, I didn't see that light. Sorry about that." And he answers, "Well, dummy, you should pay better attention next time." I can say, "Thank you, officer, I will next time. Thanks for calling it to my attention." I like that better than my replying, "You dummy. You don't need to talk to me like that. I'm a taxpayer here and a friend of the governor. What's your badge number?" then sneak over to his house some night and throw nails in his driveway because he's damaged my puny little ego.

Jackie found this attitude helpful to her in Germany. She doesn't understand a word of the language, and she was always driving around alone. When she needed something or couldn't find something she'd ask if anyone spoke English. Everyone would shake their head, "No." Then she'd say, "Gosh! I'm just a stupid American lady and I never learned your language." Nine times out of ten the Germans would laugh and tell her what she needed to know in very passable English. They didn't want to take a chance of speaking a foreign language (English) and looking stupid in front of her. They desperately needed to look right. But when they saw that she felt humble that she did not know their language, they were more than willing to help her.

My wife also had a terrible attachment to her hatred and anger toward Germany and Germans because of the war. She now has a special, deep love for the German people that she could never have found if she had stayed attached to her negativity toward all things German. She was humble enough to be taught by people she thought she hated. She found love and joy and peace with a whole country, a whole culture. It was a beautiful example to her of the power of giving up attachment to negativity.

Like the story of the Zen master and the philosopher that I mentioned earlier, we must empty ourselves of our attachments in order to make room for our spirit, in a way really, to show our mind who's boss. When the mind is in control we have no discipline. Ask any overeater or alcoholic or compulsive gambler. The nature of compulsion is in the mind and the mind will not be disciplined. The mind will tell us what we want to hear, not what we should hear.

If a person is fat and the doctor tells him he must lose weight, he tries to diet but never succeeds. The basic reason is that dieting is telling him that he is wrong to be fat. Every day, at a deep unconscious level, this fight goes on, until finally the man gives in and goes to the refrigerator. The deep relief he feels as he is porking down on his goodies is his mind telling him that he is right, he does need more food than the average person does. Even the guilt that he feels while he is eating does not outweigh his mind's need to know that he is right to be fat. His mind is grooved for food, it's been grooved that way most all of his life, and food is his deep attachment that tells him he's all right.

How does this chain get broken? It's very difficult! It takes a deep surrender of the attachment to food and a real recognition that he doesn't need to listen to his mind roaring at him for food to tell him that he's all right.

Attachments have to go. Attachments really represent an imbalance of the mind over the spirit. When the mind and the spirit are working in harmony there are no attachments. The mind isn't stuck in its grooves. The spirit keeps the mind out of its groovedness, its comparing, and discrimination. The spirit is the force that moves us toward liberation, toward wholeness and harmony with ourself and others and finally with God. It is the mind that is the antagonist. The war is one-sided. The spirit is never the antagonist, the spirit only brings peace and harmony. The spirit does not compare; it is not repetitive. The spirit is steadfast.

The spirit functions best with regularity. The mind, even though it is grooved, creates turmoil in its need for dominance. The mind's need to be right, its need to be the master, will always bring us into comparison and judgment in order to silence the spirit and to dominate.

There is no stress in a life lived in harmony. When the spirit is allowed its voice, and attachments subside, we come into a balance of body, mind, and spirit. The mind is no longer the master but is the servant it was meant to be. It is the overuse of the mind, the mind crying for supremacy, that creates attachments.

Whenever I see a person who seems overly-spiritual, a person who is walking around with every word and movement saying to us, "Look at me, look at my good works, look at how holy I am," I know that person has an attachment of the mind toward the spiritual, the so-called "holy." That is not the spirit. No one who lives in balance is obvious in what they are doing. It is no big thing. They are just sweet, quiet, gentle people who don't cause pain, who don't lay their trip on anyone, who don't see themselves as anyone special.

There is a density in people who are imbalanced. There are people who are into "the body." This again is just another attachment of the mind. Imbalance brings a density, a heaviness in everything they do. A person can be a total physical fitness nut—perfect weight and muscles all toned—yet he is not full of life. He is a heavy, blocked person.

A balanced life, lived in the spirit, brings a lightness, a flow of energy, no matter what our size, our physical characteristics, our place in life. The spirit brings a discipline that is so natural and easy that our bodies and minds just flow. The energy that is in us is smooth and easy, there are no storms around us. A person whose mind is in control is stuck. His energy doesn't flow. It comes out in storms, and then goes back into the stuck places and sits there, oblivious to everyone around him, a density, a heaviness that has nothing to do with size or weight.

Someone once said that golf is a game played in a state of grace. If you've ever watched Jack Nicklaus play golf, you understand. You can't miss his flow, his lightness. I know a golf pro who is being hurt by his density. You can feel his tension just sitting around with him. When he plays golf he is erratic. His density hurts him. It comes from the dominance of his mind's need for a good golf shot to show him he's somebody. If he felt he was all right and that his golf didn't define him, he could play right alongside Jack Nicklaus.

I recently watched Arnie Palmer play in the Phoenix Open. It was near the end of the round. He stepped up to the ball and hooked it off into the trees. He turned and said to the young pro next to him, "I tried too hard." When Palmer was young and strong, he played in a state of grace much of the time, so he didn't "try too hard."

The spirit is the unifying force of body, mind, and spirit. We are like the three-horse troika, as I mentioned earlier. When the lead horse is the spirit, the body and the mind can just key off the lead of the spirit. Some people believe that we learn to regroove our minds and substitute good grooves for the bad grooves. My guess is that this is not so. As we use meditation, as our spirit has more of a voice, we just let the old attachments fall away and the grooves diminish. When our minds decide that we are going to throw out the "bad" and substitute "good," we most often just take another mind trip. Oftentimes we end up constructing a whole new artificial world for ourselves in our attempts to "do it." Our aim should be to flow with the world as it is, not to construct our own world to delude ourselves that we are in tune with the world. When we are in balance we accept all things: all joy, all sorrow, all of the seasons of life.

We begin doing this quite simply. I am learning to do it on the golf course. I am learning to get rid of density. I'm learning to get rid of my negativity. I'm using the idea that everyone on that golf course loves me. Many times we think we have to run off and hide somewhere to learn these things. We don't. It won't work that way. We are a part of the world, and living in a nunnery or a commune or on a mountain top won't do it for us. The way we bring ourselves into balance is by practice. By being aware, right where we are.

Our biggest awareness is paying attention to what our mind is telling us. When I play golf, as I start to swing I hear my mind saying, "Watch out you're going to blow it." And now I can say to my mind, "Be quiet. I know that three out of four of my shots

will be good. And I don't need you telling me I won't be good."
Another way I try to be aware is listening to what my mind says
to me when I meet people on the golf course. This is my biggest
job. Remember when I told you that I decided when I was a
young boy that I was a poor kid from the wrong side of the
tracks? Well, what does that groove in my brain demand of me
in order to be right? It demands that I believe that people look
down on me, doesn't it? What is a poor kid doing on a golf
course? I have to practice the knowledge that everybody likes
me. Sounds simple but that's how it's done out in the world. It's
no big thing. I'm not consciously pounding on myself all the
time to "regroove." I just try to be aware of my negativity and
to substitute love instead. When I'm operating from the position
that "you like me," I'm much easier to like. I lose my density and
rigidity and fixedness. I become lighter and more approachable.

For me I need to go with the idea of getting rid of attachments rather than substituting good attachments for bad ones. I
want to get out of the grooves of the mind rather than to
regroove. I think it's just a matter of semantics anyway. It's all
just words. I need words to communicate. But I use these words
as lightly as possible. The word isn't what we're talking about.
The word is just a sign we're using to signify some general ab-
straction or approximation. As long as I use words with a good
heart toward you, you can use what I say as your servant rather
than your master. We don't want to get attached to detachment,
or attached to good attachments. Keep it light. Go easy. Heaviness is of the mind. The spirit is light and free.

I'll never forget a professor in the art department here at
Montana State University. Many years ago we were at a faculty
party together. I was talking to him and I was heavy and dense
and all intellect. Finally this guy smiled at me so sweetly and
just put his hands together as in prayer and bowed to me. There
was no offense there, he did it so beautifully. I could sense the
purity of his saying to me that he couldn't take a moment more
of my density. That was such a beautiful, powerful moment.
That man's spirit was so gentle and so sweet that it got through
my dense intellect, my terrible heaviness. I was more peaceful
from that encounter, not less. Beautiful! It was just beautiful. I
will never forget that moment, it was so lighthearted, so loving
and playful and kind.

I keep going back in my mind to the three-horse troika. When the lead horse is the mind, the other two horses, body and spirit, can't work in harmony. The body and the spirit are at the mercy of the mind and our troika is being torn apart by the wild trip. Well, how do you overthrow the mind? How do you give up attachment? It's almost impossible because the mind sure isn't going to overthrow itself. This is where grace comes in. You have to get to the point where you want to change your life so badly that you surrender.

Three frogs were hopping down a road. One frog fell into a deep, deep rut. He jumped and jumped but he couldn't get out. The other two frogs tried to help him. They got sticks and put them down in the rut but the frog couldn't make it up the sticks. He couldn't get out of the rut. Finally night came and the other two frogs realized that they had to leave their friend. They couldn't get him out. They were so sad. They thought perhaps they would figure out a way to assist their friend if they just got a good night's sleep and some more frogs to help them. So they left.

The next morning they returned with ten frogs and a rope to help their friend out of the rut. When the group of frogs got to the rut they were amazed to see their frog friend hopping down the road, out of the rut.

"What happened? How did you get out?" they asked.

"It was simple," the frog replied. "A truck came down the road and I had to get out or be killed."

And that is grace, or God, or the spirit—whatever you want to call it, however you understand it. When I see that I have to give up attachments, that I have to get out of that rut, how do I do it? Surrender. I let the spirit do it. Through meditation I get in tune with grace, God, the spirit, the old Indian on the hill, however you define it. Then I start watching, listening, paying attention to the dance of life. I see what part I have to do and do it. I let the rest be. I plant and hoe the potatoes, but don't grow the potatoes. That's the spirit. Any farmer will tell you that. We plant and we hoe, but we are not the life force. Even a farmer who doesn't believe in God knows that he does not cause the potatoes to grow.

When we plant and hoe our potatoes in the spirit, we do it just right. We don't plant to beat our neighbor and be the first one to have our potatoes up out of the ground. We don't hoe our field so that our neighbor will be amazed at our weed-free rows. We do just what is needed, lightly and gracefully. Then we watch with joy as our potatoes grow. We are not attached. We know that we cannot do any more than we have done to make the potatoes grow. It is in God's hands.

We know that we must get rid of our attachments. We also know that the only way we can get rid of attachments is by surrender. So really, what we are faced with each moment of our day is, are we going to surrender? Are we going to live in a meditative way, a spiritual way, all day long? And that brings us to our will; that free will God gave us.

There is nothing so awful as the price we pay for exercising our free will. To put it another way—doing as we damn well please. I'm coming to believe that the only thing we should use our free will for is to give it up. Give up that idea. None of us are free, we will never be free. There is a divine order in this universe, and it will not be put aside. The divine order of the universe is all-powerful, and all the pain of our lives is caused by our mind-created delusion that we can go against that.

Going against the flow of the universe is what creates sin or pain; however you define it. We use those terrible attachments of ours to tell us that what ain't so is so. We hang on to the idea that we can't get out of our rut, that our mind is our master not our servant, that we have to be fat to be right, or drunk or white, Anglo-Saxon, Protestant, or whatever.

We need to put our attachments down. Put it all down right now. Don't tell ourselves we can't. When we say "I can't" we're really saying, "I won't." Why do that to ourselves? A truck is going to come along and we'll either get out of our rut or be squashed flat. We do have a choice. It ain't easy, but it can be done, one day at a time, using meditation regularly in our lives. We will then slowly come into a balance. The mind and the body will be led by the spirit in a meditative way to bring us peace and joy and harmony no matter what is going on in our lives.

Meditation is a good way to get rid of attachments. We should always make sure that we get up early enough in the morning to meditate. This is the time we turn off the mind, the master. This is the only time we use our so-called free will. This is the time we say, "For today, I give this will to you, God. I've lived a life of free will, of ego, of mind as master, and it's given me nothing but grief. Today I will live in a meditative way. I will live in the spirit."

Every time I've been in trouble and have asked myself, "Who's causing this trouble?" it is my will that is causing the trouble. When I am doing things in the spirit, in the flow, in God's will; it pays off in real gold. When it is just self-will run riot, my payment is always in fool's gold. When it is my will going against the flow of the universe I am creating trouble for myself. I am causing myself and others pain. When I do things in the spirit it is always sweet and clean. When we make mistakes we know it. The point is to have our spirit in control so that we can admit our mistakes and get back on the track as quickly as possible. It is our attachments that delude us into believing we are constrained. We have a lot of freedom in this world, a lot of moving room when we move with the flow. The flow takes us where we belong. It shows us the person we were meant to be. It brings us the things we always wanted but didn't think we could ever have, like deep joy, happiness, peace, and content. We begin to have the abundant life that was promised us.

Chapter Six

YOU HAVE A CHOICE

That sounds like a simple statement—You have a choice. That is a big statement. The implications of it are tough to swallow. It's my experience that we go ever and ever deeper into the understanding that we do truly have a choice.

A very puzzling part of life for me has always been the question, Do we have a choice? I have found myself thinking that I didn't have a choice on certain occasions. I thought I had to do this or I had to do that. I now see that I do have a choice in most all things affecting me.

I have a choice on whether I will accept the people and things around me as they are or refuse to accept them. I have a choice on how I view my past, my present, and my future. I have a choice on which attitudes I want to have and which attitudes I want to get rid of. Even the attitude that I do not have a choice, I can now see is making the choice to believe that I don't have a choice. In fact, it is one of the most destructive choices because it leaves the person feeling locked in.

The person who feels locked in can give lots of very convincing reasons why he is locked in and who locked him in. But I see he is like the frog in the rut. Just let a truck come along and all of a sudden, he finds he has more freedom to choose than he thought he had.

I've seen too many alcoholics who believed, right up to the minute of their last drink that they had no choice, that alcohol had them in their power, and then those alcoholics all of a sudden found they had the power to get out of their rut.

To me, the most perplexing aspect of the question, Do we

have a choice? is in the area of knowing God and finding a path to God. Do we have a choice there?

It had always seemed to me that we were born into this world separate and alone and that our time here was focused on finding our way to God as we understood him so we could then find out what we were meant to be and be it. I couldn't conceive of a God who would provide us with a heaven but not let us know where the ladder was if we wanted to use it.

I could conceive of a God who allowed us complete freedom to deal with God just as we chose. I used to think that if God wanted us good, he could have made us good. Then we would all spend our time on this earth singing hymns and doing Boy Scout good deeds. I then came to see that that wouldn't be heaven; it would be the worst kind of hell. That understanding helped me to see that we all are free to cope with God in our own way.

One of the nicest ways I heard this described was by Muktananda. The parents of one of his followers were Jewish and were worried about their son. Muktananda told them they shouldn't worry because the path he followed, Siddha Yoga, was Jewish. Later that evening he spoke on this topic to the people gathered to hear him.

"In this world, there are many souls, and infinite creatures. Man is very close to God. Man has the power, the ability, to know his own Self, and to know what is inside. He also has the capacity to know God. Not only that, he has the ability to lead a very disciplined life.

"People come here from different walks of life, and from different fields. It's not that only people from a particular party or group come here. People come from all over the world, not only to this place, but to our ashram in India. Many people who follow different religions come. Some look at this with a favorable outlook, and understand it, but there are others who look at it with different understanding, and wonder whether it is all right for them.

"Every religion is okay in its own right. There may be many religions—not hundreds, but thousands of religions. Yet, how many Gods are there to bestow their grace upon all these religious people? God is one—he can't become two. Does God belong to the Hindus? Is he a Christian? Is he Jewish? Is he a Sufi? Does he belong to Buddhism? Is he black? Is he white? Is he red? To whom does he belong? This is the important question, and it is worth contemplating.

"Now, it is very likely that because he is God, he belongs to everybody. For Hindus he is Ram, and for Christians he is called God. For Sufis he is Allah, and for Zoroastrians he is Zarathustra. Everybody calls him by a different name.

"After pursuing all these religions, we should learn how to cultivate the awareness of universal brotherhood. Don't pursue these religions so that we can murder one another with distinctions. All countries belong to him, all languages belong to him, all mantras belong to him, and all religions belong to him. He belongs to everybody. All the people who follow different religions should attain this understanding.

"In America, I see people who follow different religions. A man says, 'This is my wife, these are my children, this is my dog, this is my cat,' and that is his world. In the same way, people have their own religion. A person claims that his family belongs to him, and in the same way he follows a particular religion and claims that he belongs to that religion and that religion belongs to him. God is all-pervasive. He has this vast world, and everything in it belongs to him. The entire world is his family. The earth belongs to everybody. Can God ever tell you, 'Don't go here, don't go there.'?

"I have to explain these things to you because people of different religions have conflicts. I don't belong to any religion. I belong to the religion which God pursues. God accepts everybody, and every religion belongs to him. So I also accept all religions and all religious people because they all belong to him.

"Religion itself is not God, a religion merely points God out. In our language, religion literally means *adhva*, a road or a path. There are many roads, and they are all fine, but all roads end when the temple appears. If you reach the temple, the roads have no importance. If you fight over the road, you will never reach the temple, and when you reach your destination, you will know that all roads culminate at that point.

"Ramakrishna Paramahansa followed all religions, and in every religion he found God. Man should give up this hesitation.

Man hesitates, man contracts, and because of this he fights over different religions. Then he becomes unrighteous, and he never finds God."

Many people have a hard time understanding me when I talk this way. They see me as saying their religion isn't important or that religions don't matter. We can just do what we want and everything will be fine. I'm not saying that. If anything, I'm saying the exact opposite.

Much as I have received from Muktananda, I'm not a follower of his. As he says, I'm a follower of God. The path that is the most fruitful for me is as a Christian. So what Muktananda does for me is what he wants to do, which is help me be a better Christian so I can be closer to my God. Just because there may be many paths to God doesn't mean each path isn't important. They are vitally important because those paths lead to God. When we get to the temple, we don't need the path. But until we get to the temple, the path keeps us from wandering and losing our way.

What I'm more and more impressed by is the wide range of choices that God provides for us to come to God. Many of the Jews, Protestants, and Catholics around Muktananda can't find comfort in their path and find the Siddha path is for them. Others follow that path and find it isn't for them, so they find another or return to their old path.

I believe deeply in protecting my right to seek God my own way. I'll do all I can to protect your right to seek God as you choose and if you choose. The one thing I do not believe in is trying to influence how others seek God because I believe this is the most fundamental area of choice we have.

I think the big reason we stay in the delusion that we don't have a choice is that we like being babies, and we like being irresponsible. We like not having to face the consequences of our actions. "Oh poor little me. What can you expect from little old me?"

Yet each of us see areas in our lives where we are responsible. We all ate today, we all have clothes and a place to sleep, and it is our responsibility that brought this to us. We typically have a vocation in which we're responsible. We also have avocations where we are very responsible. Maybe you make rugs as a hobby. In making those you're very careful in your selection of materials. You're very careful in the patterns you choose. You're very willing to consider the weaknesses and difficulties in your craftsmanship. In that area you are always looking for sources for improvement.

In my experience, in other areas of our life, in areas dealing with our human relationships, we are often not acting responsibly, and that irresponsibility is costing us an awful, awful price. It's just as though we are slaves. Whoever has got whatever particular thing we think we need, owns us. Our irresponsibility and babyishness ties us to that wheel that just goes round and round and drags us with it.

I had an overwhelming experience of this about five years ago. I looked at my marriage to Jackie and realized that she was the person I wanted to be with more than anyone in this world. "Yet," I thought, "if that's really true, why don't I act like it?" I realized that I was being terribly irresponsible. I acted as though I was afraid of her. I would flee from her. I was terrified of the consequences of some of my behavior. But I had to say, "Okay, if I want this marriage, I have to stand for what I believe in. I have to start being responsible to myself for my actions. I have been an irresponsible baby in this marriage."

I made a choice right there that I really had to stand up for myself, to act on what I believed in. I also saw that the results I was seeking had nothing to do with Jackie. I had to do this for me. I couldn't do this to try to control what Jackie did or get certain results from her. I had to do this so that at the end of the day I could look at my conduct during that day and say, "Was I responsible? What choices did I make today? Were they good choices, were they harmful choices?" I had to concentrate on what I was doing. I had to do my own work.

Jackie had come to some of the same conclusions for herself and was doing her work in her own way. As we each went to work on ourselves in a deeper way, I saw that this concentrating on changing ourselves instead of each other created openings for the other person, moving room, the freedom we each needed to do our own work. It created the space in which we could make more productive choices, choices that were right for us individually. This freedom led to a more realistic, more solid relationship between the two of us.

Someone asked me this question. "You said when we hurt

enough we will give up the destructive things we are doing and start to change. What can we do to quicken this process?" The way for us to see more quickly that we do have a choice, that we can stop hurting, is to see, as quickly and as clearly as possible, our responsibility for what we are doing. I have been in some of the rottenest, sickest, good-for-nothing, stinking relationships in my time. I would look at those and say, "What am I doing in this situation?" The fact I know that I am never in a situation unless I'm getting something out of it, helps me to take responsibility more quickly for my actions.

The most helpful way I know to stop a sick game is to focus all the awareness I can on the rewards I'm getting from that sick game. If I wasn't in that relationship for a reward, I wouldn't be in that relationship. And furthermore, if that reward wasn't attractive to me, I'd quit it.

In an earlier book I said that years ago I recognized I had a lot of phony people in my life. Now I never see phony people. Where did all the phonies go? One way of looking at it is we stopped being attracted to each other when I didn't need them anymore. But at a deeper level, there is no such thing as a phony. All a phony is, is someone who is showing us a part of ourselves we don't like but aren't ready to admit to yet. When I wanted the reward of feeling "put down" by all the phonies in my life and feeling terrible about it, phonies were all I saw. Wasn't that beautiful? No! It's ugly. Why didn't I quit it? The answer is I won't quit anything until I get aware of my behavior and am sick of the rewards of the choices I'm making. The faster I can get responsible and be honest about myself, the faster I will quit wanting those sick rewards.

We see this in phobias. Suppose you're a compulsive hand washer. Typically, it is a progressive thing. So while you started off like all the rest of us and washed your hands three or four times a day, soon you were up to twelve times a day. Then twenty-six times a day, then eighty-three times, then 112 times, and by the time you're washing your hands about 486 times a day you've worn the skin off your hands and you're spending so much time in the wash room you don't have time to do anything else. It starts exacting such an awful price from you that finally you seek help. You realize, "Hey, there isn't room for me and hand washing in the same life, one of them has got to go." But if you try to take a phobia that's just a mild phobia away from somebody, you'll have an interesting demonstration of how they aren't yet sick enough of that phobia to give it up. When you really get down to the bottom of it they say, "No. I can't give it up." It's just like the frog in the rut. The frog can't get out of that rut. But when the truck came along and he *had* to get out of that rut, he got out.

This is the way it is for all of us. When our behavior gets troublesome enough, when the truck comes along, we get out of the rut. You see this in Alcoholics Anonymous. There are people who thought they couldn't stop their drinking or their crazy behavior. Society didn't think they could stop either. But one day that truck came along!

I heard a story about a woman alcoholic. She thought there was no way she could stop drinking. She was also very vain about her appearance. One night she got drunk and fell in her bathroom, blackening her eye and cutting her face. The next morning she looked in her mirror and saw what she had done to her face. She went and got help for her drinking and never took another drink. That was the truck that came along. That got her out of her rut.

A lot of us see ourselves doing things we were taught as children. We aren't sure anymore that this is a choice of ours. What do we do about this? What I see is that there are a lot of our old ideas that have to go. What I pay attention to is, "Who was it who taught me this? What kind of results did they get with this idea?"

I'll pay a lot of attention to a man or woman who has an idea and is getting good results with it. I'll go a long way to study a sweet and gentle person. I watch my friend Bill Oriet in Bozeman, Montana. I watch him with himself, his wife, his children, and with the other people in the town. His ideas mean something to me.

There are all kinds of people with all kinds of ideas that are very destructive. A lot of our parents are living in the same rut that their parents lived in, and their parents before them. I came from a Norwegian family, and the typical Norwegian family wouldn't know a feeling if they met one on the street. At a funeral all they can do is shake hands and say, "sympathy," a whole line of them shaking hands and saying "sympathy," and then getting out of there as fast as they can. Now I know that they're feeling something, but they sure aren't expressing anything. Okay. That was the way of life I was taught. But my experience has shown me that this way wasn't working very well for the people who taught me. So I'm learning to express feelings. I can't care how this makes my forebears feel. It's something I have to do for myself.

This brings me to a central idea I don't believe in. A lot of people are still saying, "I'm this way because I was conditioned this way." Well, those of you who are feeling that don't have a very good understanding of psychology. My particular specialty in the field of psychology is learning and learning theory. I know how weak conditioning is. There are damn few things you can condition anyone to. Conditioning is a cop-out for most of you.

There are a few of you who had enough punishment as children, so it amounted to the kind of torture and pain that it takes to condition you. But there are damn few of you. The rest of you are using that idea to blame someone so that you can continue in your irresponsibility. Most of our learning is rewards. Life is like a candy machine. We put our money in and take the kind of candy we want. We don't stop putting our money in until we stop wanting that particular kind of candy.

To say, "I'm conditioned" is a handy way to try to say *you can't*, that you have no choice. This says that you are a slave to the people who raised you. When you are a slave you don't have to be responsible. Is that what you want? I don't think so.

At the age of about forty I started to learn to touch people. Lo and behold I made a lot of mistakes. Isn't it strange that you'd start to learn something and you'd make a lot of mistakes? Isn't it strange you can't do something perfect the first time? But I've gotten better, and I can touch people more easily now and get something out of it. I have a better contact with the human race.

I think this is important. If you learned something and it's hurting you, then do something about it. If you learned something and you're comfortable with it and it's enjoyable for you, that's beautiful. But be responsible. Look at your life. See that you have choices in what you keep and what you throw away.

It's usually in our relationship with our parents and brothers and sisters that we most have to change our thinking and recognize our choices. Say you have a brother who is always criticizing you and making you feel like you're dumb, but he's your brother. Then accept him just as he is. He has good qualities. Look for those and enjoy those things about him and quit wishing he was different. Pretty soon you'll quit noticing his qualities that you see as negative.

You wish your parents could be different with you or that you could feel closer to them. Your parents gave you the only thing they could really give you. They gave you life. Now it's up to you. Recognize that you're prisoners of your parents so long as you still think you need something from them, or so long as you just see their negativities. Look for their good qualities. They have some. They gave you life. And that was good. You're important. Make the choice to let go of the negativities. Stop being slaves to your belief that your parents made you this way. Give up your dream of what you see as perfection in a parent.

If you find this difficult, do a little research. Look honestly at your parents' parents. It will give you a perspective of your parents. You will start to see that perhaps your parents had the same difficulties growing up that you did. You might see that this rut you're in goes back for generations. Then, perhaps, you will make the choice to get out of that rut for yourself.

I'll never forget my Norwegian grandmother. When I was a little kid, she sure knew how to make me miserable. I'll never forget one particularly tough morning when we were staying with her on her ranch in Montana after my grandfather died. My grandmother was crabby each morning when we came down to breakfast. I was only nine at the time. One morning when my grandmother was especially bad, my dad took me out behind the barn and said, "We aren't going to be here much longer. It will be okay, and I appreciate what you're going through." So I have a few experiences that show me how hard it must have been at times for my mother. It's a miracle that my mother was able to be so positive and strong for me and give me the things she was able to give me.

There is an analogy to this that my friend Walther Lechler tells.

"We live in our little room. This small room is filled with many antiques—the old ideas we were raised with. We are taught from birth that all of these old things around this little room are precious. We are told how they have been cared for carefully by previous generations of our family. We are taught to care for these precious things in the same way our ancestors did so that these things may remain in this little room with us just as they are.

"We believe all that we are told, and we learn to clean and oil and polish everything in our little room and keep everything in order.

"One day we notice a small door in our little room. It's funny that we've never noticed that little door before. We ignore it for a while as we continue to do our work as we were taught. But one day we finish our cleaning and oiling and polishing a little early, and we finally cannot contain our curiosity. We go over to the door. We turn the knob. It turns a little hard, but we finally get the door open.

"We walk through the door. My God! Behind that door is a castle. We live in a castle with all kinds of beautiful things in it, but our whole family, for generations confined itself to this one little room! We are amazed as we walk through our castle. Then we must make a choice. And if we are smart, we will go back to our little room and give away everything that we don't need. We will see that we are entitled to live in the whole castle and we will tear that little room apart and get rid of the things we don't want. We must recognize we have that choice. We have the freedom to move. We don't need to take anything from that little room into the huge castle unless it will benefit us.

"The most precious thing in the world to us is choice—the God-given gift of freedom. The biggest thing that keeps us from exercising that choice is we enjoy being an irresponsible baby. Oh woe is me. Who can expect anything from me. Everybody knows I'm neurotic. I was raised wrong. I never had a chance. Mother loved the other kids best. She never loved me. Dad never appreciated me. Dad was mean to me. Dad beat on me. Everyone's got their melodrama. I was hurt bad and that's why I've done these things all my life. I don't have a choice. If my wife (or husband) knew how *I've* suffered she (or he) would know I can't do it. Maybe everyone else can. I can't."

There is a delicious joy in this kind of attitude. You can find people who will run all over you all day long to show you how right you are in your knowledge that you're a long-suffering martyr. You see someone coming and you lay right down and they run over you and, wow, it's happening just like you knew it would! "Poor Me." At night you can review all the times you were trod on in the day and go to sleep in the smug satisfaction that you were right. People are no damn good. All of your prophecies were fulfilled.

If you like that kind of reward, that's beautiful. The service you'll give to all the world is to be the resident bad example. Everyone can look at you and say, "Boy. I'm sure glad I'm not like that."

It's like Jackie says so often to people, "Christ only carried his cross for three hours. Some of you have carried your cross for fifty years." Isn't it time you put it down? This life is not about carrying the cross all your life. Christ carried his cross for three hours and then had his victory. So can we have our victory.

Some people in some religious teachings want to argue that we should carry the cross. "Poor mother (who is so mean she curdles milk) is our cross. We should carry it." No! That's not our cross, we don't need to carry it. We should say, "Mother. I respect you. You gave me life. I appreciate the many things you did for me. I will be with you at appropriate times. I will help you if you are in deep distress. But I will not carry you anymore. I no longer need to carry you. I recognize that you have nothing more to give me. I will stop knocking at your door and expecting things from you that you do not have for me. I leave my little room and go into my castle in the knowledge that what I need I will find there. I will leave my tight, constrained, limited world. I will do this because I am a child of God and an inheritor of the kingdom of heaven, and everything I need is there for me if I will but step out and claim it. I make this choice."

Do you know the hook there is in that? Do you know the stumbling block we will find if we make the choice to live in this new way? Do you know what it is that will send us fleeing back to our little room screaming, "Damn that Jess! He lied. I stepped out into the world and it was awful." I'll tell you what that hook is. It is that we want it all right now. You see the usefulness of these things I'm saying. You know their validity. But you still want to be an irresponsible baby. You want to leave your little room and have instant pleasure. You want payment from the choice without doing your work. Making the choice is just the first small step in the journey. You can't make the choice and have the pain disappear instantly. You will even have a new pain. And the new pain will make you want to run back and pick up your old pain. At least that old pain was familiar. But the new pain isn't all that bad. When you deal with pain instead of running from it, pain can even become your friend. It is your teacher.

If you really want to do this thing, if you really want to see that you are free and that you do have a choice, then start going to one of the many kinds of growth groups available to you. There are increasing numbers of these groups springing up in all our cities under all kinds of sponsorship. There are also the twelve-step groups like Emotions Anonymous or Alcoholics Anonymous or Overeaters Anonymous or Families Anonymous or Al-Anon or Parents Anonymous or PDAP (the Palmer Drug Abuse Program). There you'll meet people who know just what you're going through. Groups like this don't replace your religion. They aren't religious groups. These groups do for many of us what our churches often don't seem to be able to do. These groups are made up of people who are there because of their vices not because of their virtues. They aren't pretending you don't have to show how holy you are to belong or to be accepted. Those groups will even make you better in your religion if you have one. In church no one seems to be able to tell a story about themselves that we can identify with. But in twelve-step groups you can identify with almost every person there.

In these growth groups you will slowly come to see that you do live in a castle, because that is the only way you will be able to explain the sweetness you will come to see in the people who have been in those groups for a while. You will know from their stories that they have changed their lives, that they truly did have a choice. You'll feel it in them. But progress will come *slowly*. You will not have instant recognition, instant clarification, instant gratification. You were a long time living in that rut. And the knowledge of your freedom and your choices will come slowly, one day at a time.

Here is another story. My wife heard this story on a tape in Germany so I'll just have to tell you the story as best as we can remember it.

A king was leaving his kingdom for a year. He had three sons and he could not decide which son would rule his kingdom when he died. The king decided that he would give his three sons a test in the year that he was to be gone, and then he would better know which son should become king when he died.

The king gave each of his three sons a packet of precious seeds. He told each of his sons to guard the seeds well for their father's return.

The first son, who was very careful looked at the seeds and thought, "I know. I will take these seeds and put them in a special safe I will have made for them. I will carry the key to the safe on my person at all times, and when my father returns the seeds will be safe for him. He will see how careful I am."

The second son, who was very clever, looked at the seeds and thought, "These seeds will be old and dried when my father returns. They are very precious seeds so I will sell them now in the market place and guard the money I receive, and then next year when my father returns I will purchase new fresh seeds for him. He will see how clever I am."

The third son who was simple, looked at the seeds and went out in the garden and planted them because he thought that was what you must do with seeds. He knew his father loved flowers and was so happy when he saw how well the seeds flourished. "My father will be so happy when he sees these flowers," he thought. "He loves beautiful blossoms so much."

At the end of the year the king returned. The first son brought his father the seeds from the safe and thought, "Now I shall be king because I was so careful. A very kingly quality. I did not risk the seeds as my brothers did."

The second son brought his father the packet of new seeds and thought, "Now I shall be king. I did not return old, dried seeds to my father, and I did not risk them in the ground. I gave him fresh, new seeds. He will see my cleverness and know that I am king."

The third son took his father's hand and led him into the garden. "Look Father. Look at all of the beautiful flowers. I knew you loved flowers so much I had to plant them for you so that you could enjoy them."

The father took the crown from his head and placed it on the head of his third son and said, "What he did with the seeds he did from love for me. This is the quality the people most need from their ruler. My first son was too careful; he shows his fear.

His seeds are dead. My second son was too clever, and his intelligence is a problem to him. His seeds are not the same seeds. My third son, in his simple love for me, gave me flowers to enjoy and new seeds to be gotten from these blooms. He did this from love and it brought abundance."

This beautiful story shows us how our intellect gets in the way of our choices. It shows our fear of being held accountable for choices we make.

There is an experiment that you can do with very young children using a ring-toss game. You take a child and show him the little rope rings and show him how to toss them on the peg. You tell the child that he can stand any distance from the peg he wants. You don't prescribe a distance for the child. You will find that the children will fall into one of three categories. Some children will stand almost on top of the peg and drop the rings right on the peg. Another group will stand back a ways and get some on and miss some. A third group of children will get so far back that they cannot possibly get any rings on the peg.

Both the kids who stand over the peg and the kids who move away so far they can't possibly make it are the same kind of kid. They took two different solutions, but the two solutions were both dictated by fear. One group said to themselves, "I will stand over the top and make sure they all go on so that I can be sure to get it right."

The other group said to themselves, "I'm so scared of this I'll stand far enough away so that I'll have a good excuse for missing."

It is only the kids who stand at the mid-distance who have a high motivation to achieve things for themselves. They are aware, from the very earliest times that they have a choice, that they are free to succeed and to fail, and that it is no big thing. The other kids are already frightened and are cautious or clever. Do we need to know what is causing our fear or our phobias? I don't think that's so important. If the answers are right there and you see them, that's fine. But the important thing is doing something about it. Psychiatrists have a tough time figuring out what causes phobias. We just need to get rid of them. We need to be willing to take the chance.

So much of the time we just wring our hands and say, "I don't know what to do." General Patton told the officers under him that there was just one big rule, always advance. If you are in doubt, advance. He also stressed, as a major principle of command, that when you give an order, don't just assume the order will be carried out. Everyone around you is more frightened than you are. You have to go and make sure your orders are carried out. Because of this, you need to have your command post up near the front lines. Don't sit back a nice safe distance from the front lines and expect your men to do the fighting and take the risks for you. Stay closely in touch with what is going on.

Patton told his men this over and over again. Just before battles he would repeat this, but hardly any of his officers obeyed him. Patton had to literally go and get some of his officers almost at gun point and force them forward with their men. Patton was everywhere making his officers take responsibility.

I had a friend who was with Patton. Years ago he told me that Patton could make you mad, but in your heart you knew you were with the best fighting group in the Army. And you were safer with Patton—statistics bore this out—because he was always advancing so fast that enemy resistance never had time to form.

To me this is what we do in our lives. Like Patton's officers, we sit around and say, "I don't know what to do," but what we really mean is, "I know what to do but I don't want to do it. I'm afraid." It is fear that is stopping us. We don't want to admit our fear. We'll even lie about what we're doing rather than face that fear. We'll say, "There's no place near the front lines where I could set up my command post. This place twenty-five miles back was the only place available."

We must recognize that we're twenty-five miles behind the lines because we're afraid. It is only when we admit it that we can do something about it. Patton was discounted by some because they said that he never faced tough opposition. Patton never allowed tough opposition to form! Ask anyone who was with him in World War II. They cussed him, but they were glad to be with him, just like my friend. It's fear that gets people killed.

In Korea they did a study of lieutenants. They asked the sergeants if their lieutenant made his decisions quickly or slowly. They didn't ask if the decisions were good or bad, just if they were made quickly or slowly. They found that lieutenants who made decisions quickly had far less casualties in their companies than lieutenants who made decisions slowly.

It is fear of making a decision, it is fear of recognizing that you have a choice that is keeping you locked up in your prisons. It's not weakness! We need to have a great deal of strength to be able to continually resist progress. It takes a great deal of strength to persist in maladaptive behavior. It takes a great deal of strength to continue doing things that have hurt you so badly. Some of you have been doing things for fifty years that have hurt you terribly. That's not weakness, that's great strength. All you have to see is that you do have a choice to start using that great strength in more positive ways for yourself.

In the marriage relationship I have no patience with a spouse who comes to me and points the big finger at the other partner. I'm real uninterested in that. It takes two to make a healthy relationship, and it takes two to make a sick relationship.

I know a guy who was addicted to heroin. He started to date a girl who didn't use hard drugs. She knew he was a heroin addict, but she married him anyway. She evidently thought that her love could cure him.

After they'd been married a while, his habit was so bad that he began to wet the bed. His wife would get up and go sleep on the davenport when this happened. All of this time she was loving him and trying to help him.

One night he wet the bed. All his wife did was make a little crying noise and roll over and continue sleeping. The next morning the heroin addict had a deep insight. He told his wife, "I'm a junkie and I'm sick as hell. But you've got to be sicker than me. I peed all over you and you didn't even move. You need my love so bad, you're so dependent on me, you let me pee all over you."

Both of these people are healthy and happy today. They're still married to each other, and he's been off of heroin for nine years. Their health began the morning the addict recognized that his wife was sick, too. To the world she looked like a nice, patient, Christian martyr. She wasn't. She was like so many people who like to point accusatory fingers at their mates, who love to list all of the pain their mates have caused them. She needed all of his pain in her life so that she literally let him pee on her. I see this over and over again. I have mates come in and bitch and bitch about how miserable their lives are with that so-and-so they're married to. I suggest that if things are that horrible, a sensible person would leave a mate like that until the mate straightened out, and I almost get beat up.

No one wants to see that a responsible adult does not need my advice. A responsible person who loves himself does not need to ask anyone what to do. He knows what to do in a positive loving way. When a responsible person does something for himself it never hurts anyone else. It may look like it is hurting someone else at first, but in the long run it isn't. The long run always shows the positive effects of a responsible person making good healthy choices for himself or herself.

The question is never doing something about another person. The question always is: "What can I do today for myself?" Don't scream and complain about your mate's addiction or their alcoholism or their adultery. Don't say, "Oh, what can I do? I don't have a choice." You do too have a choice. If what you're doing really bothers you that much, admit to it and do something about it. If you don't want to do something about it, admit to that. That's a choice. And we must respect our choices.

Look after yourself. Take care of your own responsibilities. Your mate isn't using heroin because of you, or drinking alcohol because of you, or committing adultery because of you. And you aren't hanging in there because of what your mate is doing either. You each have your own personal, private reasons for what you're doing. Find your own reasons and make a choice for yourself from those reasons and your needs. That's free will. That's choice. The other is just spinning your wheels to avoid responsibility.

Wanting to change is not enough. You have to desire it with every fiber of your being and then do something about it. Finally doing something for yourself is a step for desperate people, people who are sick to their guts with the behavior they've seen in themselves, and of the consequences of that behavior they've seen in their lives and the lives of the people around them.

I cannot be specific about what you individually must do for yourselves. But I know you don't need me to be that specific. I cannot take responsibility for what you have to decide. Your choice must be yours. And I know very well how strong you are. People who persist in asking others for specifics are asking those others to do it for them. It's just the same old game, you want to stay the baby, and you fear the unknown. But behind all the reasons and excuses lies irresponsibility. You know what you need to do, and you do too have a choice.

Chapter Seven

TAKING CARE OF YOURSELF

As I mentioned at the end of the previous chapter, a lot of people ask me to be more specific and tell them what to do. In a very important way, that's being a baby. A baby needs things done for them. An adult knows what they need to do. The big difference between being an adult and a baby is that adults take care of themselves.

In this chapter, it will be interesting to see how many of you will try these things I will be telling you about. I'll bet you a dollar that a week from now many of you will find to your horror that you won't have tried very many of the things I'm going to suggest to you. And the people who always want me to be more specific are the people I'm most likely to collect a dollar from.

First of all I suggest that you find a growth group of some kind and start going to meetings. Most people, when I tell them this say, "I'm not that bad."

I myself attend a self-help group once or twice a week and have for fourteen years. It's made a big difference in my life. I first went to take my wife who was too shy to go herself. I thought that she probably needed to go, but I didn't think I did. She said that she wanted to go but didn't want to go alone and would I take her? So I did. But I didn't need that stuff. I had a recent Ph.D. in psychology, and I was voted top teacher on campus, so I didn't need any self-help group.

But there was a warmth and acceptance in that room that gave me the feeling I had found the home I was always looking for. I stayed because of that warmth, not because I needed to go to a meeting with a bunch of crazies. I didn't see where I was powerless over my emotions or anything like that. Looking back over the past fourteen years I now see that when I needed this group the most I went the least. I went once a week then. Now I go more often. This past week I went to three different self-help meetings. I don't miss a meeting lightly. I don't miss now unless there's something awfully important going on.

I find I feel better and healthier and kinder when I go to meetings. I usually go to two, two-hour meetings a week. That's four hours out of my week. In return, I figure I get an additional ten hours in my week of more efficient, better-quality time. And I feel better generally all week long. So I found the excuse that I didn't have the time was meaningless.

It was in these meetings that I first made the statement, "What troubles me is that I don't have close emotional relationships." And in the acceptance of me by the people in that meeting I saw my own lie. It didn't trouble me at all that I didn't have close emotional relationships. I enjoyed having a hundred friends so that I needn't have any. I had a hundred acquaintances so that I didn't have to be close to anybody. That insight helped me to do something about that problem in my life.

I started making close friends, and some of them were pretty raunchy. I had to have friends I could feel superior to. I had to face how low I felt about myself in that situation too. One of my first friendships in Bozeman deteriorated pretty badly. The guy had an alcohol problem and got married!

Jackie said to me as my friend began married life, "Does it occur to you that now that he's getting married, you won't see as much of him as you used to? Do you realize the only men you can have friendships with are bachelors? They're the only guys in Bozeman who are free to go hunting or fishing or horseback riding anytime you want to." There was pain in her voice as she said that, and I had to look at that too. It was true. One of my friends was a bachelor and another was married only in a most nominal way. Sort of like me. His hunting came first, second, fourth, and fifth and his wife and kids sort of tagged along in there someplace.

The important thing that helped me to see and change this destructive behavior of mine were the things I learned from the growth groups. I came to trust those people, and I then could look at what I was doing to myself and others. I could begin to relate to people in those meetings, and slowly my new way of being began to leak outside those meetings into the world. I'm not an alcoholic, but I was also able to go to Alcoholics Anonymous open meetings where I was taught the twelve-step way of life.

My wife gave me a compliment the other day. I ordinarily wouldn't include it but I think it might help some of you see yourselves and me in a clearer perspective. My wife was talking to one of our sons. This is what she said: "Son, you and I see the world in glorious technicolor. Everything in it is a huge melodrama. And that's all right. It's where our creativity comes from, but it's often made me impatient with your dad's dull plodding from A to B to C. Now I see the wisdom in it. In his deliberate way, he gets his work done, while people like you and me go dancing off ignoring our work. There has to be a balance, son. It would be ideal if you had a little more ABC and a little less dancing."

I envy Jackie's enthusiasm and magnetism and her ability to bring such excitement into living. But I am her stability. Without me she would have gone up in smoke years ago. Without her I would be a dried up little Norwegian with not much life. This difference in our two natures is where all our pain and all our joy comes from. And it is why so many people can see themselves in our stories. If you don't pay any attention to anything else I say, pay attention to this. It is obvious to me that most people don't want to plod from A to B to C. I didn't want to have to do it either; I'm no different from you. You want to look at the whole alphabet and then jump from A straight to Z. But you can't. And it is your attempt to avoid walking from A to B to C that is hurting you more than anything else. Life is not easy, but it is simple. The complication comes when we skip the whole alphabet and rush to Z. When we do this we arrive at Z full of stupidity and harmful inconsistencies that hurt us and everyone around us.

There is no school to teach us how to live, and that is a sadness. But I found my teachers in growth groups and in the twelve-step programs. I call this process Mutual Need Therapy because people are helping themselves by helping each other. So if you feel powerless over your emotions or alcohol or your eating or drugs or gambling or any other compulsions in your life—do something about it. You don't need to hurt. And the interesting thing is that these groups are free!

In life I learned to reward myself. When I was studying for my Ph.D., I would reward myself with ice cream cones. I would study an hour and then get a cone. Study another hour and get another cone. Study a third hour and then I could go home. Another reward I gave myself was a horse. I'd always wanted a horse. So I went out and bought a horse. I paid $150 for him and got an old saddle for fifty dollars more. I rented space in a friend's pasture for a few dollars a month and rode my horse up and down the pretty hills in that pasture.

It always amazed me how little it cost me to have what I really wanted. In my earlier days I spent hundreds of dollars not buying what I really wanted because I was buying for show all the time instead of what I wanted. There needs to be a place in your life where you get some things that are really important to you. Most of our deep wants are fairly simple, like ice cream cones. I have set myself up on a reward system where there are good things happening in my life. Who put those good things in my life? I did. Who's going to put some good things in your life? You are. Do this instead of sitting around and looking at everybody else and screaming, "Why don't you do something good for me?" You have a choice, and you can build some good things in your life tomorrow.

I have news for you compulsive overeaters. I personally know a woman who lost fifty pounds by rewarding herself with an ice cream cone every night before she went to bed provided she had dieted perfectly that day. She lost her weight in just a few months.

I'll never forget the couple that came to me for marriage counseling. They were miserable. I asked the guy what would he most like to do if he had three hours to himself right that day. He said that he'd like to go fishing. He looked at his wife. She told him to go ahead, she'd mind the kids. Then I asked her the same question and she said she'd like to go hiking in the mountains right out her back door. Her parents lived next door so she could ask them to baby-sit. These answers were too simple for that couple. I could see them getting half mad at me. They were so tied in to the idea they were miserable with each other that they couldn't allow themselves to have fun. It turned out later that they did get divorced, so that shows you what a lousy marriage counselor I am.

The important thing that struck me about that couple was that they didn't want to give up their misery. They didn't want simple answers. They didn't want to do something for themselves. They wanted divorce counseling, not marriage counseling. They wanted me to help them prove to themselves that it was impossible. And of course, it was.

We all do that. You do it too. The most difficult thing about going from A to B to C is there isn't much misery and there isn't much glory in it. It is so mundane nobody wants to do it. But I'm telling you that it's the only way there is. It's easy to worry about what the President will do next, or about the situation in Iran or Afghanistan, but it's not easy to hoe the potatoes or wipe the baby's butt. Yet almost all the pain you and I will ever know comes from not hoeing our own potatoes or wiping our own baby's butt.

Whenever any of us face having to give up our own pain we run away because the void we see scares the hell out of us. All I'm telling you to do with that void is give it an ice cream cone and you get so damn mad at me. Before you walk away from all that pain you want me to tell you that you deserve the whole world and everything in it. Well that isn't so. Nobody's pain is that special. Mine isn't and neither is yours.

If you start working ABC and have two or three nice things happen to you in a day, and if you have a couple of people who love you in that day, how can you come home and feel sorry for yourself? How can you come home and be nice and neurotic and miserable? How can you say, "If you were treated like I was treated today, you'd be crabby too?" You can't support that attitude when you spend a day being nice to yourself, so you're robbing yourself of a whole bunch of your fondest alibis. That's why so many of you will resist taking care of yourself.

So, build some nice things into your day. A lot of you will say, "Well, I'll try that tomorrow." No. Do it today. Either it is today or never. You know that.

When my wife came home from Germany, she told me about her birthday over there. It really struck me. In Germany no one gives you a birthday party or buys you a cake. You buy your own cake and invite your friends to your own festive occasion. You give the party!

That is so beautiful. How many of you can remember being hurt on your birthday because no one gave you a party? Every one of you I'll bet. Well, that doesn't have to happen ever again. Give your own party. Invite who you want, and be amazed. You won't have a chance to sit home alone and feel sorry for yourself though, so you'll have to decide which you'd rather do. You have a choice. You can be miserable or give a party.

I gave myself a big birthday party this past October. I had the kind of party I had always dreamed of having. I was tired of being the same little boy who was always feeling sorry for myself.

So I invited all my friends to come and celebrate my fifty-fourth birthday on October 11, 1980. It was beautiful being with all my friends at one time, and, since many of them didn't know each other, it was fun seeing them enjoy each other.

When I was calling people to invite them, Jackie asked me what I was going to do about presents. I had already thought about telling people not to bring presents, but I realized I would enjoy receiving their presents. So now I have a new red wool shirt and two knife sharpeners and a jacket and all kinds of other presents.

Jerry Sullivan's wife, Darlene, had an interesting thing to say at the party. She said, "It's so nice to be at an adult birthday party. The only birthday parties I remember were for kids where I was always one of the mothers scurrying around making sure things got done. Here I can just enjoy myself." So that was my party. And I'll probably do it again next year.

Do things like this for yourself. Spend the next seven days building one or two good things into each day. See how you feel at the end of that seven days. It will make a big difference in your life, believe me. I have good things in my life every day. I already have a whole week of nice things to look forward to. You might say, "Boy. You're sure lucky, Jess." No! I'm not lucky at all. I'm grateful for these good things, but I'm doing my part. I'm willing to let good fortune knock on my door and walk right in and sit down. I'm willing to be responsible for joy in my life just as I'm going to be responsible for my own birthday party from now on. And what's more important, I was willing to let go of my own negativity about my life. I was willing to do my own work, to be responsible.

What I'm so struck by is how deeply we have to be hit before we really change and take responsibility for what's happening in our lives. I've seen people have the deepest kind of spiritual experiences in so many different forms. I've seen people receive "Christ as their personal savior": get "IT" in EST; experience the flow of Alpha Awareness; balance themselves with Polarity; get relieved of alcoholism, neurosis, or overeating through the twelve-step programs; get a new way of life through drug or alcohol treatment; use scream therapy to get rid of pent up feelings; go through encounter and come in close contact with other people; have an affair and love someone very tenderly; use Transcendental Meditation or some other form of meditation and experience a oneness; join a religious movement and surrender their lives to that movement or join a commune and unite their lives with the lives of the group. I've seen some people that have done a number of these things, sometimes simultaneously.

The big thing I see from my observations and experience is how hard it is to overthrow the tyranny of the mind that holds us in negativity about ourselves. The rush of one of these big experiences is so strong it temporarily overwhelms the mind. I've seen people so transformed by some of their experiences that their faces had the radiance that the medieval painters were trying to communicate with their halos.

Yet so often the mind sneaks right back in. It reasserts itself and has its way. It interprets the experience, says that it understands the experience, and talks it all away. Pretty soon we are back to business as usual even though it is sometimes under a very convincing new disguise. But I'll tell you, the vitality of the experience is gone. The radiance is not there anymore.

That's why it's so important to me to see a person's face and body and hear their voice. I went to Los Angeles a couple of years ago to hear some of the leaders of the human potential movement. I knew what they were going to say because I had read their books. But I wanted to see and hear and feel them in their relation to us. The two people who impressed me most were Ashley Montagu and his wife. They were both in their early seventies. There was a quiet joy on their faces and a mischievous gleam in their eyes that showed they had found something special about life and were still experiencing what that was. So when Montagu said we should live as if to live and to love were the same thing, I knew it was a continuing experience he was talking about.

Suzuki of *Zen Mind, Beginner's Mind* has that look in the picture that's on the back of his book. I once needed a picture for the back of one of my books. I showed the photographer Suzuki's picture and told him I wanted one like that. For some funny reason, the photographer failed. He kept coming up with pictures that looked like me in my various moods and feelings. I guess it might be a while before I look like Suzuki or Montagu.

Some others who look this way are Bill Hornaday of the Church of Religious Science in Los Angeles, and Baba Muktananda and some of the people around him like Tojo, Ama, Shankaranda, and Malti, his interpreter.

What happens to the rest of us? Why do we so often find something more precious than diamonds and then gradually let it slip through our fingers? I believe it is the tyranny of the mind, but how can we stop that? I think regularity is what is so important here.

I see so little regularity in our lives. I'm not talking about our intestines. I'm talking about routine, rhythm, orderliness in our lives. We don't have regularity in our lives because we are addicted to being rich. I've got news for you. It isn't just alcoholics and drug addicts who look for "highs." We all do it. We think we can escape reality that way. Our highs take us up and our lows bring us down. We end up living roller-coaster lives where neither the false high of up or the bitter low of down is really life, just an escape. We are a people trying to escape from life, not a people trying to live life. We are brats living bratty lives because we refuse the lessons of life. Even more than our pursuit of money, we are in pursuit of escape from routine, rhythm, and orderliness in our lives. We flee the discipline of life.

Jackie is fascinated by the concept that she is a brat. I told her a story that I heard at Polarity. Jefferson Campbell was in a home and there was a little baby crying and crying in a certain way. The mother said to Jefferson, "Listen to that cry. She sounds like a brat already." Jefferson said to this woman, "Yes. She is being a brat. But she can't stop being a brat until you stop being a brat." Jackie told me it was like her whole career as a mother flashed in front of her eyes when I told her this story. She suddenly saw how her bratty ways fed down to our children, time after time. Jackie then took this simple idea and began to notice her own bratty behavior and the response it caused in those around her. Then she began to pay attention to bratty behavior in others. What she saw blew her away. She came to see that we all spend a great deal of our time being ill-mannered annoying children, and that this is in large part caused by our irresponsibility toward life. We don't want to live reality, we want to live a myth. We are brats who constantly seek entertainment. We are brats who walk through life constantly asking others to do our work. We are brats who are never satisfied with today, with this, our daily bread. We think we've got to have something more.

Read carefully now because this is important. You cannot live a responsible, reasonable, comfortable life without regularity. You need rhythm and orderliness in your life to help quiet your wild, overactive mind. This is a human need. You need a set time for getting up in the morning and a set time for going to bed at night. You need fewer diversions and more routine. You need more simplicity and less stimulation. Ideally, your routine should go something like this. Arise at six or seven, have a cup of tea and then meditate for twenty minutes to an hour. Bathe, dress for your day, have breakfast, and then go to work. Do an honest day's work, relax for an hour or so with healthful exercise, have a quiet evening meal, spend a few hours in quiet communion with your family, relax, and go to bed at ten o'clock or eleven o'clock at the latest.

Weekends should be used to be creative in a way that is different from your workday week. You should still get up at the same time and go to bed at the same time you do all week with few exceptions. You still need to meditate first thing in the morning, but then you should work with your hands to create something new in your life. You should enjoy reading or listening to music or playing at a sport you enjoy. You should have the stimulation of friends and perhaps enjoy a meal with them, or a movie, a play, or a symphony.

"Yuck! Jess is telling me to live life like my parents made me live it as a kid. I remember more than anything being made to go to bed at night and get up in the morning. I saw living in my own apartment and going to bed when I pleased as my first act of independence." How many of you thought something like this as you read these last few paragraphs? Well, that's the crux of the matter. Most of you who have children watch those children become brats when there is no routine in their lives, when they have no regularity, when their meals are haphazard and their bedtime is erratic. I put it to you, that their bratty behavior is not just because they are children but because the human animal needs routine, needs regularity, needs rhythm and orderliness for its very life.

In the movie, *Honeysuckle Rose* with Willie Nelson and Dyan Cannon we see this so clearly. The movie is light entertainment with a lot of good music on a surface level. At a deeper level the movie told the story of most of us in one way or another. It was the story of a man's addiction to irresponsibility. It was the story of a man's addiction to the highs of public adulation and the gypsylike existence of life on the road as an entertainer. His addiction to irresponsibility was costing him his wife, his son, and his sanity. It was a classic example of a life with no routine, no rhythm, no orderliness. Seeing that movie made me even more dedicated to seeking regularity. The morning after seeing that movie, as Jackie and I were talking about it, she said to me, "Hi brat." And I replied, "Hi brat," and we both laughed. It was so true!

In my first book, *I Ain't Much Baby—But I'm All I've Got*, the major theme of that book was, when I accept myself as I am, then I can change. I guess the major theme of this book would be, when I accept life as it is, then I can live it.

We cannot change life. Life is. Most of the pain we cause ourselves and others comes from denying that fact. The powerful thing I see though is when we accept life as it truly is, our own reality changes. We quit being irresponsible babies, brats really, and start becoming livers of reality instead of escapers. And to our amazement life is beautiful, and we wonder why we fled life for so long.

To become a good liver of life we must be responsible. The primary act of responsibility is accepting ourselves as we are. It's my experience that most irresponsibility comes from not accepting reality, not accepting who we really are. We construct our lives to deny the truth of ourselves to ourselves. And that is all ego. It doesn't matter if we see ourselves as less than we truly are or more than we truly are, it is all ego. What ego is, simply put, is our "being God" instead of accepting God.

So, we accept ourselves as we truly are. Then we become responsible for that. I am a writer who is writing this book. Is this a perfect book? No. This isn't a perfect book. Perfection isn't reality. When I desired perfection, when I wanted 100 percent of myself, I couldn't write books or do anything else. I accept the 90 percent plus I can achieve in this book, and I take responsibility for that. Am I going to be destroyed if a few people write letters to me and tell me about some fault this book has? No. That is them doing what they think they should do. That is their opinion. I must not slip into irresponsibility and let what others think or do affect my doing my work. Now, if I were locked into the irresponsibility of perfection, criticism would destroy me. Instead, I look at a criticism and see how it applies to me. What good can I get out of it for me? And I have enough responsibility to laugh at myself. I do not take myself as seriously as I used to.

Another act of responsibility is to see what our needs are and then to fulfill those needs. It's very important to find the things that really mean something to you. As I said earlier, my horses mean a lot to me. I now have five acres of land, and so it is easy to have horses. There's so little grass that I need to feed hay most of the year. But I can have my horses around me. In order to have my horses nearby, though, I didn't go crazy and buy a hundred acres. Most of our real needs are simple to fulfill, but when we are locked into negativity we take simple needs and find a way to make them complicated and therefore impossible to fulfill. That is our game, and that is irresponsible.

I have six horses now. Some of those horses were gifts. Doctor Jim, the horse that I ride all the time, is the colt of a mare that was given to me. A friend gave me free stud service, so Doctor Jim is free top and bottom. The mother of Doctor Jim recently had another colt, a filly we named Phoenix Joan. She was born when Mt. St. Helen's erupted and dumped ash on our place, and Jackie and I had just returned from Phoenix. Also, because a Phoenix is a mythological bird who rises from the ashes, we thought Phoenix was a good name. I love my horses, they give me pleasure, the sweet pleasure of fulfilling a need.

From the pleasure of fulfilling this need I have so many additional pleasures. Our home is in the middle of the pasture. I can look out a window and watch those horses play. I can see them get skittish when a storm is coming and watch them frolic with each other. They're like watching kids playing.

There's a lot of good things in my life, and all of them I let God put there. A few years ago I met Jefferson Campbell of Polarity. He's a vegetarian, and so I thought, "Well, I'll try vegetarianism just to get the feel of it." Right away I lost a hunk of weight I'd been trying to get rid of for a long time, and I felt better. So I'm sticking to being a vegetarian, not for religious reasons or anything like that, but just because I feel better.

Since changing my eating habits and losing some weight I can do better when I go hunting at high altitudes in the snow and the cold and I don't get angina anymore unless I do something especially strenuous. Yet, despite my heart, there are a lot of the so-called healthy guys in Bozeman who can't do what I can do. Of course, I don't act like a kid either. My brother comes out hunting in Minnesota and shoots an elk, and right away he starts wrestling with that elk and is going to move it all over by himself. Men my age who don't accept limitations are in danger. They could kill themselves. I don't move an elk around. I tie a rope to the elk and then to my horse and my horse moves the elk. A lot of the advantage I've got is knowing my limitations and staying comfortably on my side of those limitations. I'm no King-Kong, and I don't have to prove anything anymore.

In this chapter, I'm telling you all to find your needs and fulfill some of your needs, and do some of this every day. I know that a lot of you won't. Not can't—won't. When we say "I won't," we show our neurosis.

A neurotic is a person who can screw up a free lunch. A neurotic is a person who is good at snatching defeat from the jaws of victory. A neurotic is a person who can consistently think his way to defeat. A neurotic is a person who will not fulfill simple daily needs because he's always chasing rainbows. A neurotic is an inflexible person. A neurotic chooses a thousand small miseries trying to escape some nebulous big misery that might or might not happen. A neurotic is an angry person who wants company in his misery and so lives a self-fulfilling prophecy; he creates chaos and misery in his life.

A neurotic person will not do something for himself. He paralyzes himself by continually creating defeat because he expects too much from himself and from others and from the world. There is no simplicity in neurotic people. They and their whole world are very, very complicated. You have to complicate yourself and the whole world to create so much misery for yourselves! Sane, rational people can be very complicated too, but their complication comes from their many facets, and there is an order to that kind of person. A neurotic is complicated chaos.

What I love about the twelve steps is what they have taught me about living. Those twelve steps bring an order to that mess I had created. In the early days of our life, when Jackie and I were deep in our respective neuroses, we didn't know what kind of people we truly were. I always thought I was simple and she was complicated. Now we see that the opposite is true. She is simple and I have many, many facets. That was an amazing revelation to both of us. In order to find who we truly were, we had to take the risk of throwing away our neurotic selves. We both had to be willing to throw away our whole past lives and all that we thought we were in order to find out who we truly are. This is everyone's spiritual quest. Locked in neurosis, we cannot make our spiritual quest, we can only live in delusion, trying to escape our real and our imaginary pain.

Most of our pain is self-created. Most of our self-created pain comes from our neurotic delusion that we should not have any pain, whether it is physical pain or psychic pain. The truth is that a lot of life is pain. Until we recognize that and embrace our pain, learn the lesson it offers, and treat pain like the old friend it is, we spend our lives fleeing. Joy and pleasure are parts of life too. But did we ever learn much when everything was great? No. We learned from our pain. And when we learned the lesson of that particular pain it went away. Then another pain comes. That's it. That's life, but we don't like that deal so we choose to try to hide from pain by using pills or alcohol or drugs or food or work or coffee or cigarettes or a hundred different things outside ourselves. We cut off our feelings and live in illusion and delusion.

A long time ago I heard a friend talk about giving a problem a "spiritual treatment." A spiritual treatment is looking at a problem and saying, "Okay, how is God in this problem?" The more you give a problem the spiritual treatment, the less it is a problem because you come to see it is ego—us trying to be God —that is causing the problem. Ego creates a lot of problems. Ego magnifies problems by telling us we shouldn't have this problem. Giving a problem the spiritual treatment gets rid of the ego.

Another treatment you can give a problem is the gratitude treatment. A priest named Father Martin has a beautiful expression about gratitude. He says, "Gratitude is the silver platter we hold out to God upon which he can give us new gifts. Ingratitude is the halitosis of the soul."

I find it very fruitful to focus upon all the things I have to be grateful for. Ingratitude is choosing negativity. Gratitude is choosing to find the spiritual basis behind all of life. Gratitude is realizing that there is a God and that his will is in everything. In my wife's book, *I Exist, I Need, I'm Entitled,* she tells about her terrible pain when she finally realizes the total depth of her devastation. Walther Lechler then tells her to be grateful for all of her pain because all of that pain brought her to that moment. There is no physical pain that I know of that can equal the psychic pain any of us feel when we finally hit bottom and see ourselves and our whole life as it truly is. That moment is horrible. But gratitude is the only proper reaction. Yet we live most of our lives choosing to be so ungrateful for our lives that gratitude is not a virtue we have much familiarity with.

When you are ungrateful for the weather and can't see the whole picture, you can be miserable on a sunny day in Phoenix in the wintertime. I saw this while I was there. My wife and I had traveled down there fresh from eighteen inches of snow in April, so it was easy for us to be grateful for the weather. But we often found Phoenix people crabbing because the wind was blowing or because it was hot. I'm sure someone from the arctic ice cap would wonder why we wanted a vacation from just eighteen inches of snow. Ingratitude is the inability to see the whole picture and to realize that we are just a small part of that picture, we aren't the whole show.

What is it in our present situation that we can be grateful for? There is always something, even in a death. We can be grateful for what we got from that person while they were alive. When we focus on negativity, when we have no gratitude for our life, we exclude all of the lovely things that happen in our day. Ingratitude pushes away life. Ingratitude is a little death.

One day Jackie and I witnessed a stupid senseless act. We were driving to a seminar in Phoenix and we were talking about what I was going to say, when Jackie spotted a man with two huge rocks in his hands pounding dents in the hood of a car. He went over and did the same to a second car and then walked into his yard obviously yelling at someone. It was so senseless and insane to witness this it made your stomach hurt. His negative act made both of us feel very negative for a minute. Deep in neurosis we could have let this man's negativity cause us to ignore the palm trees swaying in the evening breeze. We could have gotten so caught up in that melodrama that we wouldn't have been able to relate to the people who had come to be with us. We could have taken his violence and used it to remember all of the times we had done something that stupid. But that would have been an ungrateful thing. Gratitude means seeing reality.

We didn't know him or what had made him do that. We were just passersby. First of all, we were grateful we weren't that angry. Then we were grateful those weren't our cars. And then we were grateful that we didn't belong in that scene. Gratitude is the attitude that everything is precious. And gratitude shows us what we can do and what we cannot do.

"Why does it always rain on my parade? Why, just when I am driving by does this man throw a temper tantrum and upset me, frighten me, and make me think of my own anger and bring it boiling up to the surface?" You see? It's very easy to be negative, but negativity is a big pain. It hurts your stomach and gives your face an expression like a pickle. Frown lines get to be pretty permanent after a while. They get etched in deep.

When we are angry our body is flooded with the hormones that helped our ancestors flee from the saber-toothed tiger back when we lived in caves. In anger, our whole physiology is turned upside down, and that is what kills people with heart attacks. A type A person, a heart-attack-prone person, is filled with free-floating hostility. He can get angry at anything, he's just waiting for a place to attach his hostility all day long.

Okay. That's me. A type A, heart-attack-prone person typically has a loud voice. When I worked at the university Jackie used to call over there and ask if I was in. Sometimes the secretary would say, "Well, I haven't heard his voice in the halls, so he must not be here." My voice was so loud she could hear me talking three offices away.

Today, my voice is much softer. People don't hear me talking a long ways off. I used to be proud of my big manly shoulders. Whenever I bought a suit it had to be cut away below the collar in back because my shoulders were so high. Later, I learned I had tense shoulders, not manly shoulders. My shoulders have dropped an inch or so lower now at the points of my shoulders, and I can buy suits right off the rack with no alteration. These changes came about as I began to take responsibility for what I was doing, change what I could in my life, and practice an attitude of gratitude.

A long time ago someone wrote me about what they had read in *Hey, God, What Should I Do Now?* This person said, "Jess, I think some of your heart problems are coming out of nutritional problems." I treat the letters people write to me with respect. So I read that letter, and I asked myself if there was validity in that comment. This person recommended that I get in touch with a doctor who is famous for his understanding of the relationship between nutrition and disease. I contacted that doctor, and the result is that I listened to what that man said. He didn't prescribe specifically for me but he told me that he felt that many of my heart problems and my floating hostility were coming from my reaction to sugar. So I quit eating sugar. He recommends a high-fiber diet for his patients, and I did that for myself. Then he recommends high dosages of certain vitamins for his patients. I ordered those vitamins and began taking them.

I am the owner of my body. I am responsible for my body, and I made a commitment to honor that responsibility. My body is beginning to show the positive consequences of my improved maintenance of it. It's just like a car, when you take good care of your car you get better performance. I still suffer from some of the consequences of my old irresponsibility. Some of that can't be undone. But I'm not adding to the problems anymore. I've had a pacemaker added to my previous heart surgery, but that was because of that early damage to my heart, and I've finally seen that it is my responsibility to do what I can to see to it that

I'm not careless with the maintenance of my body anymore. And from the work I have done over all these years, and the grace of God, I've had a great healing.

When we begin to see our responsibility to ourselves we begin to recognize how careless our attitudes have been, and changing those attitudes means that we must deal with ourselves on all three levels: body, mind, and spirit.

My wife sees this so clearly in herself. She wrote in her book about how she gave up the use of chemicals. Now she is dealing with other attitudes she had about eating and smoking. She's scared to give up the cigarettes until she's lost all the weight she wants to lose. Yet she told me one day that the cigarette smoking is coming out of the same attitude the compulsive eating was coming out of. She said, "Food, coffee, cigarettes come from the same idea that tranquilizers and anti-depressants and booze come from. They come from my belief that I need to take something outside myself that will make me feel better or still my pain. I know, Jess, that I'll never lick the food binges until the cigarettes go. And I'll never lick the cigarette habit until the food binges go. As long as there is one shred of that old attitude left in me, I'm just one step from having a slip back into using again."

She has told people that she'll never truly be her right weight until she gives up cigarettes, too, and yet few people will encourage her in this. They show her by this attitude that they don't understand what she's saying. I hope you see what she is saying. Until we have a spiritual awakening to the depth that we are truly reborn, not just phony reborn, there aren't any of us any more than a small step from slipping back into our old ways.

I'll accept the electronic help of my pacemaker, at the same time recognizing that a part of me wants to cry out, "Why do I have to have a pacemaker? They're for old guys in their seventies and eighties." And I'll also practice gratitude that someone invented pacemakers so that my heart can beat a regular 72 beats a minute now. I'm grateful that the pacemaker helps to give me rosy cheeks and helps me do a lot of things I couldn't do otherwise. I'm grateful for its protection in those times when I really need it.

When you begin taking responsibility for yourself, you aren't going to be very far along on the trip when the magnitude of what a big job it is begins to sink in. Because, when you begin to take care of yourself you all of a sudden realize that it involves a lot of others besides you.

I had to realize that I had to let Jackie and my kids go. I had to quit having expectations about what they were going to do for me. A lot of men have heart attacks and die because "sonny" didn't come into the firm. That's true! There's a study that shows many men have heart attacks soon after a major disappointment with a son. Dad's a top-flight lawyer and sonny becomes a dope-smoking hippie. Dad has a heart attack when he realizes that sonny isn't ever going to cut his hair or go back to college, at least not in the foreseeable future.

Jackie realized that she was justifying her continued use of prescription drugs because of what our kids were going through and because of what I was going through. She had to put us down. I wasn't asking for that kind of power over Jackie, and our kids weren't either. She put us down and liberated herself from us, and it had a powerful effect on all of us, believe me.

When you start to see that taking care of yourself means just what it says, you free yourself from all the people who've been your excuses. The outcome of that decision is to give the people who have been your excuses more freedom, too. Those around you then have to continue with their own things because they choose to and not because they're reacting to something in you. It's that old teeter-totter concept. It takes two people balancing their weight to keep that thing going. If one person shifts his weight or gets off the teeter-totter, the other person must shift, get off, or find somebody else to teeter with.

A lot of times when you decide to take care of yourself by getting off the teeter-totter your partner is going to get mad at you or try every old trick he knows to get you back on that thing with him. But that's okay. You don't have to do it!

There's one way a lot of people in our society today aren't doing a very good job of taking care of themselves. That's in their use of sex. They have the idea they need to have sex a lot or they will go crazy. They can't see that it's their abuse of sex that is the problem. What they are taking for their problem—sex —is the problem. From what I've seen, sex works well on a long-term basis only for people who are legally married. Yet so many people with so much misery in their lives want to tell me how important sex is for them. I'm not impressed. So a very important part of taking care of yourself is in using your sexual energies very carefully.

Taking care of yourself also means paying attention to how you spend money. Most people live in an economic rat race of their own creation. I met a guy once who wrote a best-selling novel. I'll never forget him. He was making maybe $50,000 a year as an advertising man when he wrote a big-selling book. He was involved in the sale of his book to the movies, and he was all excited about it. He said, "Jess, I'm going to buy a Lear Jet. I've always wanted a Lear Jet." I said, "Wait a minute. You don't know how much you're going to make off of your writing in the years to come. You don't want to get your standard of living cranked up so high that you're going to have to work like crazy to keep going." He just laughed at me. "I'll write another book," he said. Well, he didn't write another book. He's back in advertising, which he said he hated. I really loved that guy. He had a way of saying things. One time he said, "Jess, your writing is so rough it makes my eyelashes fall out." That's true. Some of my writing is that rough! But because of not living at a reasonable level, he's back writing advertising instead of books. Now, maybe he belongs in advertising more than in books. I sure hope so. But I've still got the time to write books because I kept my standard of living down where I could afford it.

Most executive types can't do their jobs and be effective and still have anything of themselves left to bring home at the end of a day. The really smart people who have learned to take care of themselves find work that satisfies them so they come home with lots of energy left for being with the family. Their job gives them enough money to put bread on the table with a little left over for fun, and they enjoy life. They do their eight hours in a job that doesn't suck them dry, and they haven't cranked their standard of living so high that they're worried sick all the time. They're taking care of themselves in a good, healthy, responsible way.

It's just crazy! I'm continually amazed by all the people in America who go out and buy the biggest house they can just barely afford and then sit around living in the misery they've created by buying this house. Some of these people come crying to me about their misery and I say, "Do you need that big house?" And they think I'm crazy not to see that they can't be happy in anything less than that.

A bishop of the Catholic Church flew from the East to spend a night with us a while back. He said to Jackie, "I'm enjoying the simplicity of your home. It's good to see that you have kept your life the same way."

Jackie wanted to laugh at him, but she didn't. She could see that he was so used to going into people's houses that were a lot fancier than ours that it amazed him that Jess Lair, writer of books, lived in this little house. Jackie knew right away he had assumed we had a lot more money than we have. We're not millionaires and we aren't going to buy something to pretend we are. We went that route a long time ago, and we paid the price in worry and debt and strain. We learned that lesson. For us, it's got to be simple because we value freedom more than anything else.

We go to Phoenix in the winter and live in an 8' by 21' trailer. It gives us two of our basic needs, shelter and freedom. Jackie and I need that more than we need the strain of another big place to worry about. Sure our egos could give us some problems because of the way we live! But we have to have freedom; that's what's important to both of us. When you have love you can live in a little trailer. When you're hating each other you could have a house that's four hundred feet by eight hundred feet, and it still wouldn't be big enough.

You can't buy something to impress your friends with either. That isn't friendship. You don't intimidate friends. If you're going to park a matched pair of white Cadillacs in your yard and then go looking for companionship, you're going to have a tough time finding true friends. That's what I love about a friend of mine named Roman. Even though he's rich, he isn't ostentatious.

All of these things fit into doing something for yourself. I'll bet a lot of you think you have to keep working awfully hard, but if you rearranged your financial priorities, you wouldn't have to work near as much. If you love your house and are happy working hard because your nice house is a basic need of yours, that's great. But don't complain about the high price; just enjoy working for it. That's taking care of yourself, too.

It is important to recognize that you are a three-dimensional animal: body, mind, and spirit. You cannot separate them. This is a mistake so many people make. They think they are going to work on their bodies, and then they'll be healthy. Or they think they'll be all right if they just straighten out their minds. Or they think that they'll be fine if they become more spiritual. None of this works. When you desire a true healing, you must heal all three aspects of yourself or you will not be healed. Body, mind, and spirit. Three distinct different parts of you, and yet all three are hooked together.

In Western civilization we tend to sort and separate things so much. We separate the mind and the body. Well, they're not separate. The body is crystallized mind. I'm sure all of you have had the experience of looking at someone and realizing that his state of mind is written all over his body. In other cases, it's obvious where a person is spiritually when you hear him speak or look at his body.

When you exercise the body it helps clear the mind and lifts the spirit. When you clear up your thinking it sends better messages to the hormones that activate our bodies. When you develop a spiritual life the mind clears and the body feels better. They're all three hooked together.

Taking this system and using it to work on just one aspect of yourself will not work. You might get into physical fitness and temporarily clear your mind and delude yourself that something permanent has happened. But it hasn't.

Or you might take the route so many people have and get into the mind. You might think that positive thinking or using EST or something like it is the answer, and again you have a delusion because you've done nothing for the body or spirit. And soon you're hurting again.

Another route that I see so many people take is to get into the spirit and then, wow! Because it's from God and so socially acceptable, it's got to be the answer. No. Again it's not the whole answer. These people are the hardest to deal with because they're so deep into being holy and they're so self-righteous about it. These people seem to suffer the most because they are so frightened. It's so hard for them to see the terrible limitation their supposedly holy trip has placed on God. And under it all they are so frightened and so angry and defensive.

People who go into the body or the mind keep seeking, always seeking. People who go into the spirit often don't dare even hint to themselves that it isn't enough. People who go into all three aspects begin to truly live their God-intended life, and they are so quiet about it that most people are unaware of them for a time. But soon you can't help but realize that something very real and very deep has happened to these people, and we all begin to beat a path to their door. Do you know what these people do then? They smile. That's all. They just smile. They don't talk of their experience, they don't teach or evangelize, they just live.

This is why it's been so hard for people like me to learn the way to go. I always thought it was the teachers and the preachers and the psychologists who were going to show me the way to go. Now I see it's something different than that.

The way I see it is that we all have our own unique spiritual quest to make back to the God of our understanding. This quest is accepting the three-fold nature of our humanity and taking responsibility for ourselves, and finally allowing ourselves to heal ourselves, body, mind, and spirit.

This is the package. When you start the commitment to take care of yourself you have just begun a life-long journey toward life. You have just stopped your life-long journey fleeing from life. You have begun to see that you are the captain of your ship, and only you can guide it by giving up control of the ship to God each morning and going along for the ride.

Chapter Eight

MARRIAGE IS FOR PAIN—AND GOING
TO GOD

I used to think marriage was for happiness and joy. The only problem with that idea was that when I wasn't in happiness and joy in my marriage, then I figured something must be wrong with my marriage or me or both.

I have come to see that marriage serves a far different purpose than I had understood before, and that purpose has nothing to do with the kind of happiness and joy I thought I was seeking. The kind of happiness and joy I was seeking was where my wife made me happy, I made her happy, and the marriage made us both happy.

I see now there is no real happiness that way. And I see that the real happiness comes in a very different way. For me, the real happiness comes from wholeness and being in union with God. That happiness brings the other happinesses as a side benefit. But seeking God and union with God and wholeness guides me into areas I never sought when I was just seeking happiness for myself and my wife.

The understanding I have of marriage is that it is a triangle with God at the point of the triangle and the two partners on the legs of the triangle moving up along those legs toward God. The purpose of marriage is to let us have a close relationship where we are completely vulnerable. In this close, vulnerable relationship we are able to see ourselves as we would never be able to if we weren't married.

The way I see life, as I'm saying throughout this book, is that we are born separate and alone and that all of life is our search for God as we understand him. If we see this, then we look at marriage or the celibate life and decide which path is for us. Pope John made his voyage to God by himself without a marriage. I long ago decided that the married path was the path for me.

I chose to enter into a relationship with a partner of the opposite sex. As I am in that close relationship, all kinds of parts of myself are exposed to me. This is a great source of pain to me. But I see now that this is what I really needed. Out of the pain of self-knowledge and self-discovery that is in marriage, I am gaining the deep and lasting happiness of coming more and more into union within myself, with my fellow humans, and with God.

So that's why I see now that marriage is for pain. I need a marriage and a marriage partner who will bring me the maximum in self-knowledge. I need a marriage that will break down the crust of my ego. That hurts but any healing starts with the healing crisis—the high fever before the fever breaks.

There is happiness in marriage for me, but that isn't a problem. By seeing that the crucial part of marriage is the journey to God and the pain of self-knowledge that takes, I can handle the hard times in the marriage. Now I don't see those hard times as a sign of failure, something I need to run away from, but as a sign the marriage is working, doing just what I wanted it to do.

When you look at marriage this way, you have a great tool to use. As one of my friends put it one time, "Marriage is a life-long healing crisis." That's true because no more do we solve one problem than we are faced by a new one that we are now strong enough to tackle. The times of happiness in between pain get better and deeper and last longer. But right up to the end there will be the times of deep, intense pain. Or, at least this is the way it seems to me now.

A friend of mine once told me this story, and it brought tears to my eyes. Our role in life can be likened to being hitchhikers. We get out on the road of life and stick out our thumb and somebody picks us up. After a while that person says, "This is as far as I go, I'll have to let you out now." We get out on the road and stick out our thumb. Another person picks us up and takes us for a while, but then once again the message is: "This is as far as I go, I'll have to let you out now." We repeat the same action many, many times with many, many people. Finally though, someone comes along and says, "I'll take you all the way." The thing that takes us all the way is the path that leads us to the temple. The longer we've been out on that road, the colder and hungrier we have gotten, the more we are open to being willing to "go all the way," and the more willing we are to see and understand the spirit in its many guises.

Some people sometimes become alarmed at my seeking. They think that I am a spiritual dilettante. Well, I'm not. I have my basic group that I answer to, and I have a path and a basic program that I adhere to, and whose discipline I submit to. Every new idea that I look into is looked at from the context of my basic program and its principles.

Life is a process, and all of the people and events in our life are a part of that process. They are the rides we get along our hitchhiking way. It is always interesting and funny and strange and weird and beautiful how God works. The minute I came to the writing of this chapter on marriage, God proceeded to give me lots of experiences. Up here in little old out-of-the-way Bozeman, where Jess Lair, this little Norwegian kid lives, God sure didn't forget about him. God just reached down and gave old Jess some things to work on because he was going to write about marriage.

It was a Tuesday in September, a day I'll never forget. I managed to have a bill come due on some actions of mine the previous week. I really screwed up. I was able to do something that *grievously* offended Jackie. One of those, "This is the last, last, last time" things, you know? And of course in my horror I had to see myself very, very clearly. I saw my tremendous lack of awareness, my tremendous stupidity. In fact, if I told you my story, not a one of you would believe it. It wouldn't sound possible that someone could be that stupid.

I was hurting so bad from what I had done that I instantly became physically sick. It was just a disaster. And I had done it all myself. I couldn't blame my wife for contributing to what I had done. I was all alone in the doing. Jackie and I had to go up to Great Falls the very next day to tape a television show on our books. We both had to smile and act like nothing had happened. I saw how I had contaminated Jackie's very first appearance on her new book by my blindness and stupidity.

Jackie asked me somewhere during this time if I was really ready to write this chapter on marriage. I said, "Sure! My humbling experiences will sure keep me from being arrogant when I write this chapter."

While I was suffering so from this thing I had done, I got up one morning and was reading a book that had been sent to me by a publisher. In this book there was a chapter on marriage. The author had described the beautiful marriage she had. It was so idyllic. This woman had quoted me extensively throughout her book, and I had wanted to write her a letter and tell her something that someone once told me. "Too many quotations and footnotes are a distraction in a book." I wanted to tell her that once she had taken an idea in from my writing and digested it, it was then hers to say in her own words, and she didn't need to be constantly giving me and others credit lines. I saw it would be hard to write what I had to say, so I decided to call her instead.

In the course of our telephone conversation I told her how fortunate she was to have such a beautiful marriage, and how lucky she was. Then I mentioned that my experience in marriage was very much the opposite of hers because I had lots and lots of disadvantages when I started that were preventing me from achieving that kind of overwhelming success that she was writing about. And her voice broke! She said, "I'm glad that I wrote that when I did because it isn't that way now."

So, things had gone all to pieces for that woman. It was so fascinating, not because I wish ill luck to anyone, but because it was just another indication of two things that I have observed. The first thing is that all of us have problems, some have more and some have less, but we all have them. Another observation was that this Christian lady, through gritted teeth, wanted those problems to go away—right now! She asked me, "How long is this going to go on?" I said, "I don't know. Maybe twenty or thirty years. How long is cerebral palsy? How long is the death of a child?" Another thing I noticed about her is that she wanted to direct all of her hurts toward her husband. I told her, "Hey, honey, don't do that. You look at yourself. Let him look at himself."

I hung up from that phone call with an odd feeling. I was sorry for that woman, but still half-amused at seeing the real truth. I've never yet seen the marriage that was as perfect as the one that she had written about, and it turned out that my observation was still holding true.

The next day I came down with a cold. I almost always catch a cold when I'm stressed. And this time I was going through agony at what I was facing in myself. So—there I was with a cold, a stomach that was distended, and rumbling, full of pain and agony, and I suddenly realized that I was feeling exultant, fantastic, because things were so tremendous.

How could things be so tremendous and my body not know it? Things were so tremendous because I finally had the experience deep in my guts of a self-knowledge that up until then I had only acknowledged in my head. My wife had told me that I was doing this type of thing, sending out these messages, and she hit me with enough evidence that my Norwegian mind had to acknowledge that it was probably true. But the nature of the mind, as I said earlier, is to be grooved into self-justification, and while before I could always acknowledge the evidence, I readily also thought about reasons and justifications for why it wasn't all my fault. "Not little old sweet innocent Jess!"

But here I was. I couldn't wriggle out of this one with excuses or blaming. I had done it, and the pain to me and to Jackie was overwhelming. And it was a relief to face it experientially, and not just by someone's say-so.

Everyone who reads this can tell me from their minds that in the final analysis of our lives it is not the results that we should be interested in. Rather, it is what we do with what we have that is important. What we know in our heads is helpful, but what was so important for me in this experience was that I had the absolute experience; deep in my gut, through to my soul, of what I had done. And I knew that I was responsible for what I had done. I couldn't weasel out. Then I found I was ready for the second and more deeply responsible step of seeing myself realistically in my marriage.

The beginning of this deeper knowledge came with the realization that marriage too is a process, just like life, and we are not answerable for having "the perfect marriage," but we are answerable for what we do with what we've got. The experience was part of the process, and I was now ready to be responsible for what I learned from it.

The deepest part of the experience for me was that I was able to put down my guilt and my fear about what I had done. It is guilt and fear that paralyzes us and keeps us locked into our old behaviors. When I go out on the golf course, if my family's life and happiness depends on my getting a par 4 on the first hole, what am I going to do? I'm going to blow it. There's no way I can get the ball all those yards down the fairway, up onto the green and into the cup in four strokes. By the same token, if Jackie's life and well-being depends entirely on my never making a mistake, then what does that say to me? It says, "Watch it!" to everything I do.

I recognized that most of the problems I created in our marriage came from my own deep need not to make waves; to get A's in everything. And this very feeling was causing me to make mistakes, to be careless and fuzzy in my thinking because I couldn't carry the load. My kids were always saying, "Lighten up, Dad." Jackie talked about my "heavy attitude." My old attitude was a burden that was smothering me and making me flee my wife and family in many ways because there was no joy in it. When there's no joy, everything and everyone is an obstacle.

My wife didn't cause me to have this attitude, and neither did my kids. But as I made mistakes, their reactions were strong enough to make me feel worse and worse. Neither my wife nor any of my five children are what you might call weak-willed people. I've often said to Jackie, "We prayed that our children would have minds of their own, and God sure heard our prayer." As they reacted we all would dig deeper holes for ourselves. Now, on this morning that was so powerful in my life, I was set free. I had done something that deeply affected Jackie, but I knew, I experienced the knowledge, that I had to deal only with my part of it, and that her reactions, however justified, weren't mine to deal with anymore.

What does this say? Am I copping out on the hurt that Jackie felt through no fault of her own? No. I am just saying that I can't make Jackie feel better about what I did. I can't take away Jackie's pain. I can only deal with what I did and how I felt about it. I faced up to it that morning that Jackie had every right to divorce me. If she did, I would survive. I knew I didn't want a divorce, but I also knew I couldn't be in the position, any longer, of trying to stop Jackie from doing what she felt she had to do. In the release of just carrying my own responsibility, and not trying to outline what Jackie did about it, I was able to see what I had done more clearly and what I had to stop doing more clearly.

None of us can ever see our irresponsibilities clearly when we are terrified of what others will do or feel or think about what we have done. This kind of terror causes more and more mistakes. People who live this way are like the proverbial bull in a china shop. Most of the things we do are clumsy and blind. We are blinded by our own false sense of responsibility and behave in a way that looks irresponsible as hell to those around us because we are always in reaction to what we fear others will do or think or say.

Did Jackie divorce me? No. She was mad as hell and had a lot of pain and confusion for weeks. She thought I was copping out on her, making ultimate excuses for what I had done. She thought I had an ego that could twist and justify any damn thing I wanted to, and that she was a fool to stay with me. For herself she saw that this was the final straw, and she would never let me hurt her like that again.

She decided to give it a month and to try to learn to unhook from me emotionally. That was a disaster, I'll tell you. She saw that emotional detachment from me was not a marriage. It was just two people living like strangers together. Jackie has always had a deep intuitive belief that "emotions are the voice of the soul" and whenever the emotions are smothered or subverted, the soul is in agony. My wife has strong feelings about this because of her experience of life and from things she learned for herself and wrote about in her book. She is aware that her deepest anger and contempt has always been toward people who create artificial worlds for themselves in order to control their own and others' emotions. She sees these kinds of people as "dangerous babies," in her words, and so she quickly found out that she could not shut off her emotions toward me, or quit caring about my emotions.

After thirty-one years, neither Jackie nor I take divorce lightly. We have watched too many marriages break apart in these times, and haven't observed that anyone is any happier after it is all over. So she decided to look at what I was saying and to apply it to herself. Suddenly she saw that she had been doing the same thing I had. She, too, was always reacting to how things affected me and what I was thinking and feeling about her, and this was causing her to do a lot of things that were hurting me, too.

I started out in marriage with as little qualification as you can possibly have. It's a great tribute to Juckie's patience that we are still married after all these years—a modern-day miracle. It's also a tribute to me that despite these disadvantages I have been working my butt off for these thirty-one years. That's what marriage is about.

I want to switch here and tell you a story about elk hunting. It's related to marriage as you'll see. This story is about three situations in elk hunting.

The first situation is about an elk hunter who took up hunting but for the first few years didn't get any elk. But slowly he got good enough to get elk regularly and to see them a lot. He got good enough to start walking up on elk in the trees and went from being a stumblebum in the hunting business to where he was very successful as an elk hunter. He got good enough to have other hunters seek his counsel and association.

The second situation is about a guy who had a heart attack quite early in life and then took up big-game hunting. In his first years in the mountains this man had to carry an epinephrine "wheezer" with him all the time because his breathing was so bad. He couldn't walk very far so he had to hunt mostly in places he could drive his jeep to, and then he had to sit and just wait hoping an elk would walk by. After a few years this man had to have a pacemaker to help his heart, so he had the doctors put it on the left side so that the recoil of his rifle wouldn't damage his pacemaker. After a few years the first pacemaker wasn't working right so he had to have a new pacemaker put in on the right side and so this man had to learn how to shoot left-handed. And any of you who shoot would know it isn't easy changing an instinctive, lifetime habit. This person with these tremendous physical handicaps was still persisting and doing some elk hunting each year.

The third situation is about a person who was a tremendously result-oriented person. Results were everything. He was tremendously concentrated on goals and accomplishments, so much so that this person was very poor company for the people around him. This man had the experience in mid-life where he realized that his brother, who didn't have much money, had a deer rifle and this man, who had money, didn't. The fellow thought, "Well, even if I had a deer rifle I wouldn't have the time to use it, and my brother does. And worst of all, even if I had a deer rifle and the time to use it, I wouldn't have anyone to go with me, and my brother does." Things changed for this man over a period of time so that he became very little result-oriented, and the experience of the hunting process became a joy for him. It wasn't just the hunting itself, it was the thinking and planning, the enjoyment of getting together with friends to plan and pack up, the horseback riding, and everybody setting up camp. There was pleasure in striking camp after the hunt and getting home and telling the funny stories over and over again, and looking at the pictures taken on the hunt. It was all part of a lovely process.

What is interesting about all three stories is that they're all about the same person. Me! This drastically, physically handicapped person is shooting an elk each year and is enjoying each part of the process and having fine companions to hunt with. And furthermore, I don't care whether I get an elk each year or not.

When it comes to elk hunting I'm a tremendous success. I'm a tremendous success in relation to where I was and what I had to work with when I started out.

What I saw so strongly in marriage is that we have to look at marriage in the same way. We must see that we take what we have and do the best we can with it and let go of our goals of seeking "perfection" in marriage. As Miss Piggy says, "You gotta go with whatcha got." I'm not the knight in shining armor who can give Jackie everything and spare her everything. I believe that us men expect that from ourselves as much as women expect it from us. This attitude causes a lot of pain and anger and self-hatred and recrimination that needn't be.

I'm not going to have to answer to God for the state of my marriage. I'm going to have to answer to God for what I did with what I had. (The old "talent" story.) The more I see this, the more moving room I have. It's that moving room we give ourselves that can take a goal-oriented, physically handicapped guy who can't shoot worth a damn right-handed and turns him into a happy, successful, left-handed hunter who bags an elk every season and has fun in the process no matter what happens.

I put this spiritual awakening that I had about myself and marriage on a par with the spiritual awakening I had at the time of my first heart attack when I said, "I'm not ever again going to do anything I don't believe in."

I haven't met many people who are meant to be celibate. There aren't many Pope Johns around. His path to God was obviously the celibate path because the joy and peace and power of that man still echoes in our hearts nearly fifteen years after his death. As near as I can see, most everyone is meant to come to God with a member of the opposite sex, and in a sense, through the opposite sex.

What I have seen about relationships is that it is only in relationship that we can find out some very important things about ourselves. Most relationships serve the function of lifting us up and bringing out the best in us. If our friends don't do that for us, we drop them and find friends that do. There are only two kinds of relationships that function to help us see ourselves more clearly and speed us on our spiritual path. One relationship that does this, amazingly enough, is our enemies. The other relationship that does this is the marriage relationship. Our mate tells us about that part of ourselves that we don't want to see. No matter how loving our relationship is with our partner, he or she is the one person on earth who knows us the most completely. Even our own parents never knew us as our mate knows us. Immediately, when you put it this way, we can all understand divorce better. It is usually a result of people experiencing more pain and self-knowledge than they want and can handle. Seeing this gave me a better understanding of divorce, and I come from a heritage that is totally anti-divorce.

The nature of man is to be responsible, and the nature of woman is to be receptive. There are a lot of problems nowadays because men are so irresponsible and such babies that a lot of women are reacting in one of three ways, all unreceptive. Some are saying, "Hey, I can't stand any more of this. I'm going to split and do something different." Some others are reacting more strongly and saying, "To hell with men. I'm going to be both a man and a woman in this woman's body. I can sure do a lot better job than he can." Still a third type of woman is looking around and totally refusing the experience of marriage. This woman is saying, "No way! I don't want to have anything to do with anyone masculine because I've seen women who've been dominated and brutalized and every other damn thing, both emotionally and physically, and I won't even entertain the idea of marriage." So both men and women are denying their nature.

I'm going to include here a piece on marriage my wife wrote to me once as we were puzzling this out. I'm sure you'll find this interesting. I know it made me sit up.

MARRIAGE

So I said to my wife . . . "Jac, what is a man?" And this is what my wife replied.

"I can't tell you 'what is a man.' But I can say how I see you and what I think that you must do for yourself now.

You're nearly fifty-four years old, Jess. We've lived together for thirty-one years. We've lived through a lot of joy and pain with each other and with our children. When I think of the fire we've come through so far I do believe we are very rare metal.

I've watched you, Jess, these past three years since you returned to me from your seven years of seeking. I think every man alive goes through a searching time, and you were no exception. You had to go in search of yourself, of what was right for you. In our society as it was constructed when we were young, you finished college, married me, had five children, worked hard and dropped of a heart attack at only thirty-five. How could mid-life cause you to do anything else but seek a better way?

When all was said and done it was me you chose again. You said it was because I am the most interesting woman you ever met. This is true. I am a very interesting woman. You never bored me either. You are far from dull.

Most marriages, in our age bracket, go through a crisis time. And better than half of them survive. It is the quality of the survival that worries me. Most of them survive by going their separate ways yet living in the same house. The personal encounters become subdued and quiet and dead. They settle for peace at any price.

There is that within you and me which cannot settle for peace at any price. We have both lived too close to the fire. It would be better to go our separate ways than to smother our fierce tenacity.

Jefferson Campbell at Polarity Institute taught you that a man is responsible and a woman is receptive, and that marriage is a lifelong commitment. He told you that you and I are on a journey toward God and that you would make a mistake in leaving me because you would find that you would have to go through the same pain with another woman, no matter who she was.

I will now tell you how I see us in light of what Jefferson said.

He is right. A man is responsible and a woman is receptive. And a man must learn to accept responsibility. It is an awesome thing, and few men ever achieve this. Man's irresponsibility gave rise to women's lib. Women are angry; justifiably so. They are waking up, along with others who have been oppressed by irresponsibility.

I have slowly come to believe that it is possibly true that we live many lives. I have no difficulty believing this and being Christian. It doesn't make sense to me that we get only one lifetime in which to learn all that is needed to become one with God.

You came back into my life three years ago a man who was committed to our marriage, ready to be responsible, and that was good, in essence. But a man who has girded his loins with responsibility and commitment is a terrifying visage. My experience with you has been that you did not come back committed to me, but committed to the idea of commitment. Through gritted teeth you were saying to me, "This marriage is a commitment, I am going to be a responsible man and I will act responsibly and manage our affairs in a better way, and be home with you more, and behave myself, and do things I have seldom done like mowing the lawn and paying the bills and tending to business. Now you be receptive, goddammit."

And I must look at you, Jess Lair, and say that this is still the same old scene, played over and over again in our marriage. Everything that you do is done to set me apart from you. Why do you fear me so? What is there about women that makes you so angry? Why do you flee me?

I am woman. I am your other half. I am that part of yourself that lies sleeping inside of you. You wish to stay married to me? You want me to make a commitment to stay in this marriage? You don't want me to ever again say, "I don't know if I can stay with you, Jess Lair"? Then you stop fleeing me. I say the words, "I do not know" . . . but you do the fleeing.

You want to stay married to me, Jess Lair? Then surrender to me. I am you. A man can never be whole unless he becomes his other half. Look at me, Jess Lair. I am you. That *you* that you seek, yet run from. Ah God! All men are the same. They need us, they want us, yet they flee and oppress us because they cannot see that they will never be whole until they are consumed in us, until they become us, their other half.

Run, flee, do your numbers game, your intellectual, scientific, unemotional, smothering trip. Have your heart attacks, your strokes. Die, and then do it again. And the day must come when men must see the distinct possibility that they cannot go to God except through woman.

What is woman to man? An exquisite torture chamber that he must go through to be perfected. Look at me, Jess Lair. I am strong, I am gentle, I am kind, I am the spirit of man. I am in tune with the earth, with children and animals, with flowers and birds and trees. I know my joy; I know my pain and sorrow. I know fear and sadness. Oh God! such sadness. And yet I am faith, the almighty, powerful belief that it is not all for nothing. That life is all beautiful.

You men, you say these words, you want to believe, but you do not feel. And you never will learn to feel and know deep in your soul, until you embrace your women. Until you become your women.

A woman is receptive? That is a nice intellectual concept. Do you have the courage to know what receptive is? To be receptive instead of intellectualizing it? Intellect. I spit on intellect. Man made intellect their God out of fear of their own spirit, which is woman.

Receptive is to become one. Receptive means to take a thing inside oneself and feed it and care for it and let it become a part of you until there is no difference between you—even if in doing this you yourself are destroyed. And that is the power and majesty and awe-inspiring, God-like quality of woman.

Women's lib will fail, as it is now, Jess Lair. Do you know why? It is because women mistakenly think that the way to liberation is to become like man. How can they be so stupid? Women's lib is an acting *against* instead of *for*.

Women will be liberated when man is liberated, and not before. I will be liberated when you surrender to me and allow my receptivity to consume you and make you one with me so that there is no difference between us. And in your surrender my surrender can come. But you must face the fact that man's responsibility does not just lie in doing outward things, in paying bills and mowing lawns and being involved with your family. Your awesome, terrible responsibility is to turn and recognize me. Woman! Your other half. Your responsibility to yourself and to me is to become me. ME!

I have watched many men die prematurely and alone, with their family on the sidelines. I know many men who have chosen death though they still live. And all of them are dead because they will not become whole. And their wives and children will never be quite whole because of their irresponsibility.

I am in awe of men. I see them as they are truly meant to be. I see them in my mind's eye as they were meant to be, though I have only experienced two men who have even begun the journey toward wholeness. But knowing and experiencing them was enough.

It makes me mad to say this, I don't wish to think it is so. But perhaps, if it is true that we live many lives, our last life *is* lived as a man. Yuch! As a woman this is hard for me to say, because you know it means I must go around again—if it is true. I say this though because of what I see in men. And what I see is an awesome thing.

Man is here on this earth to become whole; finally and irrevocably whole. Woman is here on this earth to teach wholeness to man. And the terrible dichotomy is —woman cannot teach what man will not learn. The closer man is to finally learning his terrible lesson, the angrier he becomes, the more he must resist, and the sooner he grabs a disease and succumbs rather than finish this trip.

Woman is simple. Man is complicated. A complete man, however, is remarkable in his simplicity. Simplicity is his hallmark. The hallmark of a whole man. Why do I say this? Complication comes from resistance, and resistance comes from man. Woman is simply woman. She must not become other than she is else she cannot fulfill her role in this tragi-comedy. She is complete as she is. But a man cannot become complete and simple until he takes upon himself the awesome and ultimate responsibility of surrendering to woman and being consumed by her and in turn consuming her.

Read your Bible. Read of Eastern religions. Read your history books, Jess Lair. They all teach the same thing. The story is always the same. Woman is life. Man is death. And here and there the great ones appear. And the great ones are always men who are more like women though they are the most awesome, powerful, earth-moving men who have ever lived. They are men who changed the world, yet they did not go to war, they did not kill, they did not hate, they did not defile. Their power was acceptance and integration and love. They were men who were receptive as well as responsible. They were men who carried their woman-side within themselves and functioned well with it.

Look at Jesus Christ! I believe that he was God made man. He was receptive to all of life. He had the love of a woman for her baby at her breast. He had the compassion of a woman kneeling at her dying husband's bedside. He had the acceptance of a woman giving her last crust of bread to her hungry child. He had the faith of a woman lying on the ground to give birth to her child. He had the patience of a woman waiting for her man to return from war. And all of this he integrated with the power and glory of his responsible manhood. The simplicity of his wholeness reverberates still. Men like to think about his God-hood forgetting that he also showed them man-hood.

Look at me, Jess Lair. Look at Woman, Jess Lair. We women are an awesome thing for we are the spirit of man. And because you aren't Jesus Christ, and you weren't born whole and complete and simple, you must come to me. You must not resist me anymore. You must take the final step of ultimate responsibility and step into me, for I am you. You chose me as your other self thousands of eons ago, and that is another awesome terrifying secret of woman. You cannot do it without us. We will always hold power over you and send you fleeing until you grow up enough to die to us. Man's surrender to woman is the beginning of his journey into the spirit.

When you surrender to me will you become like me? God forbid! Who would want to be like me? Only I am me. No! You will not become feminine. You will become only more of what you already are, a masculine man. Ask any woman alive. A truly masculine man is not a macho man. He is a gentle man who is loving and kind and tender, but awesomely responsible. A surrender to me does not mean that you take on my negative qualities either. It does not mean that you become anything like me. Only more and more like yourself.

I've met many men who are very powerful in their worlds. I have observed that most of them get their power from resistance. They have great negative strength, and it is consuming them alive. They are cannibalizing themselves and everyone around them in order to resist becoming whole men. They think women are on earth to give them birth, to decorate their homes, and to try to steal their genitals. And it is because of men like these that I have come to see that most men symbolize death.

It is because of two great men who loved me that I say these things today. Because of these two men I was able to see man. It's odd, Jess. One man was very old when I was very young. The other man is young now that I am getting old. But they both showed me the same thing. They showed me who I was, and in that learning I saw who they truly were. I know that it is my experience of those two great men that is being said to you right now. Those two men were so whole and complete that they became completely one with me. They saw me as themselves and treated me that way. They knew me as not even you have known me though you have lived with me for thirty-one years.

No, Jess! It isn't because they didn't live with me. It is because they became me. They were man enough to be totally ME. They knew my negativities even more truly than you do, but they knew that wasn't me. What I am saying to you, is that they became my essence and so I could become their essence. They were man enough to know that they must dive right into my soul in order to be one with me.

Don't you see, Jess? That is the secret of the terrible power of man. It is why man has always been awesome, despite what woman in her fear and lack of faith would wish to believe. The power really does belong to man. But man can only find his power through his woman. Not women. His woman.

A woman is simple, I say this again. She is receptive. She is the receptacle. She is energy, she is life itself. She is the storehouse of man's yearnings. She is his wisdom. A woman is a mirror to man of himself. And because men are babies for the most part, they go on destroying themselves and turning to woman for the food they are starving for.

It is in sex that I see man at his worst. Do you know that only masculinized women have sex indiscriminately, with no commitment? Deep in her soul, every woman knows the sacredness of sex. Women who have sex with many men have given up on men. Their sex is a denial of their power, of their receptivity. And the fact that there are women who deny their souls in this way is due to man's irresponsibility. Such is the awesome power of man.

I stand in front of you, Jess Lair, my feet planted firmly in the earth and I howl to the very heavens above, "Man! When are you going to be one with me? When are you going to surrender to me and become a whole man. If you do not understand what I say to you right now, I will die alone and unfulfilled, and probably have to do it again. Hear me, for God's sake. I can never surrender to you until you first surrender to me. It is through me, to you, to oneness. You must finally accept your ultimate responsibility. Throw yourself away, in me, and set me free. I know it. I was born knowing it. That is woman, the knowing. But it is the doing that is man's responsibility. Don't you see? You stupid man, don't you see? I am here. I am receptive, but it is you who must do it."

Men will always deny us, fear us, run from us, analyze us, computerize us, sexualize us, and even kill us rather than face that we are them and that man must be responsible for that.

There are always women who will wait. When you have been on this trip a thousand times you learn the waiting. There have been a few old souls like Georgia O'Keefe and Anaiis Nin in today's time, who are so used to the waiting that they have a completeness that even you men cannot deny. The way I recognized them is in their work. They, of all women today, make their statements *for* rather than *against*. They love men deeply, and if I only had their power perhaps I could make you see me as I see you, as they see you.

Do not listen or believe women who say, "I do not need men. I can do it myself." They are women who quit being women. They have no soul. They are too young yet, though they may be old in years. They are masculine women and will die barren. Old souls who have known love as I have known love know they can never go through the fire alone. They know their oneness with man, and so they wait, once again, for the man with the insight to say, "Hello, my woman. Let us become one and go through the fire. I see myself in you. Together the fire will melt us into one and carry us through this time, through to what lies beyond our understanding."

And then Jackie shook her head and laughed and said, "There. That part of my work in this marriage is over. I will not say this again. The rest is up to you." And she went into the kitchen and started doing the dishes.

And I began to think about what this woman said, this woman I am married to.

I am sure you all can see that I meant it when I told you that I don't have a weak-willed wife. When Jackie wrote that, she was writing it to me, but she was also writing for all like-minded men and women. She and I are learning about marriage through our own lives, not just through marriage manuals and psychological journals. And the pain of it is real, believe me!

When you start understanding and are finally able to define "What is a responsible man?" you see that this is a man who sees his nature, who understands that he is a man, who knows what a man is, and is living it to the very best of his ability in all areas of his life. Then you realize that there aren't very many examples of this around. I know I have a hard time finding many in my town. You begin to see the problem. If a boy wants to be a good baseball player, he doesn't have to go very far to find a good example—television and magazines are full of them. If you want to be a successful businessman you can study a lot of examples of that easily, too. But if you want to be a responsible, complete man, it's really hard to find lots of good examples. So I don't have any criticism of women for the difficulties that they have with the irresponsibility and babyishness of men (most notably myself) that I see.

As I've been studying in this area I have found great value in accepting the idea that man's nature is to be responsible and woman's nature is to be receptive. I first heard this theory in a clear way from Jefferson Campbell of Polarity Institute. The idea is not new, but his way of telling it struck me. The closer I come to understanding this idea in depth, the stronger I believe in it. But the stronger I put this idea to audiences, the more marked the reaction. My God, the black looks that come over the faces of these men and women. Some of them could fight me to the death, I threaten them so.

We laugh and talk about "the battle of the sexes." It's no joke anymore, is it? I've watched the looks on the faces of audiences as I have been talking about these ideas. When I talk about how men are irresponsible babies, the women begin to grin. You can just see them stretch and come alive.

When I talk to an audience about closed, hard, unreceptive women, the men begin to stretch and grin and come alive. But when I tell men it is part of their game to keep women unreceptive so that they can stay irresponsible, they don't smile anymore. When I tell women that it is part of their game to keep men irresponsible so that they can stay unreceptive, the women get mad. We all want to blame the other person. That's our human nature.

What I am talking about goes back so many generations now that there is no cause for blame. The solution can only lie within individual couples making individual decisions. There is no magic formula to change the human race.

The theory about man being responsible and woman being receptive is that as a man becomes more responsible a woman can become more receptive to the man. As they each become more of their basic nature, then the man finds receptivity toward woman and life growing within him. And a woman finds her responsibility toward men and life growing within her.

We are all—man and woman—meant to be both. A man is primarily responsible and secondarily receptive. And a woman is primarily receptive and secondarily responsible. But both aspects of each of our natures has to be working and accessible for us to be whole and complete.

Jackie can't teach me to be responsible. She can only be receptive to my taking responsibility. This is hard for her to do. She and other women have suffered for generations because of man's irresponsibility. But Jackie came to see that there is no other answer because all around her she saw "responsible" but unreceptive women raising irresponsible children.

When anyone is in a role that is contrary to their nature, they do many destructive things because they are fighting so hard to believe and justify what they are doing. When a woman has been left by an irresponsible man with the sole responsibility of keeping a home together and raising a family, that woman's whole identity is wrapped up in doing that job. She has to defend it any way she can. She can't afford to trust men. She feels too much is at stake.

How does a man become responsible? We can't teach our women to be receptive to this. We become responsible by doing it even though the woman at first may be unreceptive. We become responsible by facing the fact that we have blown it, by not condemning ourselves, remembering that there are not too many examples of this around, and then recognizing it's time to grow up. In doing this within our families some of us will find relieved, receptive women. Others will find themselves in the greatest cat-and-dog fight of their lives. But when you look at what is at stake, you begin to understand all of the confused, angry, resentful, ineffectual young people who have no alternatives but irresponsibility and unreceptivity facing them in their future.

The truth, as nearly as I can see it, is that an irresponsible man is totally unreceptive to women. In the home this is destructive for the children. An unreceptive woman is totally irresponsible toward men. And this too is destructive for children. Continuing this destructive path is devastating when we look at what is really at stake. But the alternative is so sweet. A responsible man becomes receptive toward his wife. A receptive woman becomes responsible toward her husband. The children of that marriage have the best chance to become whole and complete.

There is nothing more beautiful for a child than to grow up with two parents who are one, whole and complete, responsible and receptive in both their natures.

My wife and I intend to write a book on marriage soon with the working title: "Marriage: A Spiritual Affair." It will take a whole book to spell out to you what I have touched on in this chapter. Jackie and I both shake a little when we think about writing this book because both of us have seen that we always need to experience what we later write about. But all of our books have taught us individually more than we have ever taught others. So we will write that book. I'm responsible for that, and Jackie is receptive to it.

Chapter Nine

GETTING CLEAR AND HONEST

Clarity in our lives comes from awareness, awareness of who and what we are and seeing honestly how we are relating to all the people around us. So here we will talk about self-honesty and awareness so we can first be clear with ourselves about ourselves. Then we can be clear with others about ourselves.

Most of us are very unclear with each other. I'm very aware of how unclear I am with Jackie because I live with her so much. One thing I always did to her was ask questions. I would say, "Jackie, do you want to go to a movie tonight?" That isn't clear. What should I say? "I want to go to a movie tonight, do you want to come along?" or "I want to go to a movie tonight and I want you to come with me." Either of those two questions are clear. If I'm asking Jackie to go to a movie for any other reason than because I want to go to the movie myself, I'm not being clear, it's a half-truth question and either answer she gives me will make me feel bad and make her look bad in my eyes. If I just say, "Do you want to go to a movie tonight?" and Jackie says, "Yes," and I don't really want to go, I feel bad. If I say, "Do you want to go to a movie tonight?" and Jackie says, "No," and I really wanted to go with her, I feel bad. What does this say about this kind of question? It shows irresponsibility and lack of clearness.

A man told me of talking to the woman he was close to. He told me he asked her, "What do you think the chances are that we will get married?" Look what an unclear statement that is! Look at all the fear he shows by hiding what his feelings are and the fear of what hers might be. He doesn't say, "I want to marry you," because he doesn't even know that within himself. Even if he did, he would be afraid to put out his feelings that openly for fear of being rejected. Worst of all, we say and do unclear things like this because we want to continue our sick games that have been so much a part of our lives.

It isn't until we've really gotten plenty sick of those sick games that we'll give up that unclear communication and go to a really clear statement of what we mean. But we can't do that until we've honestly looked in our hearts and know what's there that we can be clear. That much honesty requires a deep awareness of ourselves.

One of the most difficult things in the world to live with is a person who never expresses his own wishes but asks you what your wishes are. People who do this all the time make other people the "yea" and the "nay" sayers, and then are often resentful about the yea or the nay. When we are clear and when we say things clearly, there is no reaction between us. We deal straight.

I used to think that the best teachers were the ones who had the students flocking to their offices. I don't believe that anymore. Those teachers have either confused their students or frightened them or made them dependent or are seeing themselves in a popularity contest with the students and faculty. When we know our subject clearly and tell it clearly, with no hidden messages, there are no questions and no hidden messages. The students listen to what they paid hard money to hear and then leave to go to another class. That's clear, and when we are clear there are few difficulties.

Before we say anything we should be clear inside of ourselves. I'll never forget one time when Jackie and I were going horseback riding in the early morning. Jackie said to me, "Be sure to drink some orange juice." I did. An hour later, high in the mountains, Jackie got mean and cranky and finally almost passed out because her blood sugar got so low. What she had done was to tell me to drink orange juice for her. Her body felt the need for orange juice but she didn't pay attention to what her own body was telling her for herself. She passed the message that was for her on to me. I drank the orange juice but I would have felt fine without it. She's the one who had need of the orange juice, not me. Jackie does this a lot. She tells me to wear a jacket when she's cold. She tells me I look tired when she's pooped. We're aware of this now. When she tells me to drink some orange juice I ask her if she wants some and she always does.

A lot of mothers do this. It's the old "I'm hungry, you eat" syndrome. This has made a lot of kids fat.

One of Jackie's fondest memories of her own mother is when her mother's sweet tooth would start to nag her, she'd make fudge for the family. Her mother would invariably get the giggles while she was beating the fudge because she knew what she was doing. She was basically pretty clear about why she was really making fudge.

When our wires are crossed it's usually fear. When I am indecisive and dance around and ask Jackie if she wants to go to a movie, I'm showing her I'm afraid of her and she senses that. Isn't that stupid? If you start to pay attention to the way you ask questions, you'll be amazed how unclear you communicate to the people in your life. Our communication has so many hidden agendas, but those who hear us are aware of the hidden agendas and they react to it.

Jackie has an interesting way of stating why she asks an unclear question of me. She says it's "because I enjoy the anger and resentment that I feel when I don't get the answer I didn't ask for." That's clear isn't it? She admits that she goes for anger and resentment sometimes.

We have to be clear. Some of us have had to recognize that more clearly than others, but we all have to do it. We have to recognize that we all get paid in life for everything that we do and that we pick the payment. When we pick anger and resentment as our payment, we'll feel it. When we pick praise or blame for payment, we'll know it.

Many of us are not clearly aware of the fact that we have chosen our diseases also. A person who chooses to be a bystander in life is choosing to be paid by feeling helpless and hopeless. Most cancer patients have this kind of personality. When we choose to be hard-charging, aggressive, take charge people, we choose anger and resentment as the payment. That is the personality trait of people with heart attacks and high blood pressure for the most part. The facts are clear. Now we have to be clear. Changing our personalities by ourselves is almost impossible, but knowing what we are doing to ourselves can help us to prolong our physical health and enhance our mental well-being. And it can help us see the need for a higher power in our lives who has all power, enough power to give us the spiritual awakenings that change our personalities.

This chapter evolves very clearly from the previous chapter on marriage. It's the further evolvement of responsibility and receptivity, because one of our big lacks of awareness is about our being a man or being a woman.

As I said earlier, about four years ago I realized that I was probably the world's biggest baby. I was forty-nine years old and weighed 195 pounds. The world's biggest baby!

I was in a marriage because "nice guys don't get divorced." I was there because of "what will people think?" I thought I couldn't get through a day without Jackie to cheer me up and cheer me on and make me feel good. It was no marriage. It was a dependency in practically all forms. And I had to realize how frightened I was of hassles and troubles and working things out. So I was constantly running away from the reality of our relationship. That was very unclear. I was giving Jackie the very strong impression that I couldn't stand her and that I was not willing to do my own work in marriage. That was a very legitimate impression on her part.

So, I said to myself, "I'm going to start doing my own work." I see now that I decided then to become fully responsible for myself. That was a very crucial decision for me because it helped me be clear about what I was doing and why. It had a whole bunch of tremendous results. For all practical purposes, starting from that day, I could go to bed at night and sleep the innocent sleep because I had done my work each day to the best of my ability. My conscience was finally clear for the first time in our marriage. I had stopped being a dependent baby with my wife. It was a tremendously necessary thing for me.

Taking that responsibility was the first step toward being really clear with Jackie and receptive toward her. A man who is receptive without being responsible is just weak and for the most part angry and blaming. He goes wherever the wind blows, fleeing his pain. I saw that real strength and real masculine receptivity came out of responsibility.

Now, it is my belief, that women are different from men! I

may be Norwegian, but I'm smart enough to figure out that women are different than men. And I see a lot of women, because of their pain, running from that. It is my belief that the woman who can be receptive to men, and is willing to develop that receptivity is ultimately responsible for her womanhood. And this kind of woman, then, has all the power that many women are seeking today.

Here I want to stress that this is a philosophical idea, a theory, that I have found is helpful to me. You are all lovely people reading this book, and you paid for this book. If this idea is not beneficial to you, that's fine. Just skip this part and keep going on with your life the way it is. I won't debate ideas with you. I'm just offering my idea for any usefulness it may have to you.

My opinion is that a man's personality must begin with responsibility and then come to receptivity. A woman's personality must lead with receptivity and then come to responsibility. When my fear of making waves and causing hassles caused me to appear to be just a receptive blob, I was not being a responsible husband or father, and my apparent receptivity was disguising a horrendous anger and frustration toward Jackie and the kids and life in general, and they all knew it. All of us always know everything that is going on in our family. Even the youngest child.

Jackie, for her part, was at home being responsible with gritted teeth while I apparently "played" (in her eyes), and any receptivity that was hers by nature died through the years. Jackie and I and all of our children paid a terrible price for this exchanging of roles. We don't condemn ourselves or each other for this now. Who was there to show us the way? We did the best we could with what we had under some tough circumstances. Now we are both awake, and we are changing in our relationship to each other and with our children. It's never too late to change. And although our children are adults now, they can't help but benefit from the change in Jackie's and my relationship. If they choose not to, that has to be their responsibility as adults.

In all human relationships, for all of our life, we are responsible for doing the best we can with what we have. My wife and I could look back and weep at our stupidity, as I'm sure a lot of you could. But what good will that do any of us? Will our children or our mates benefit if we run and tell them that we see now that we did this and that wrong and we're devastated by it? No. If they're anything like us, they don't even want to hear about the past. All any of us want to see is changes—NOW. So many people get an insight into past mistakes and then let the insight paralyze them further. Don't do that to yourselves.

The quotation from my first book, *I Ain't Much Baby—But I'm All I've Got*, that meant the most to people and that is most often repeated to me by readers is:

> For what I am today—shame on my parents.
> If I stay that way—shame on me.

As adults we could change that to:

> For what I am today—shame on my lack of awareness.
> If I stay that way—shame on me.

In this new awareness that Jackie and I have come to in recent years, we see many ways that we are so beneficial to each other. I've often said that I wouldn't know an emotion if I saw one. Jackie is a deeply emotional woman. She is teaching me about emotions. On the other hand, my lack of emotionality offers Jackie some stability that she wants. I've seen a beautiful play back and forth between those attributes we each have.

A lot of women, in today's society, because of being around a lot of men who are irresponsible babies, have been grievously hurt. They are wanting to keep the reins in their own hands because they have given up on men. They don't dare trust anymore. Many of these women feel they were forced into this position even against their own choosing. Some other women were raised by mothers who felt they had been forced into this position before them and who taught them that they had to go it alone, and these women, unconsciously for the most part, chose their irresponsible baby to marry so that they could continue on the way they learned. Both of these types of women are saying, "I will control my own and my children's future because I dare not trust in the future to these terrible irresponsible babies. I will be primarily responsible." And they lose touch with their receptive natures. This is an imbalance.

I now wonder if there is any connection between this decision on the part of so many women and the sharp rise in cancer in women. One thing that makes me think that there is a connection is that we have some psychological evidence that cancer is essentially a "hopeless and helpless" disease. And breast cancer seems to have some relationship to not being sure about one's womanhood. I saw one study where a psychological test given to women the night before they were going into surgery for breast biopsies was able to predict with about 70 percent accuracy whether the lump was cancerous or benign. The essential ingredient the psychological test used to predict the women with cancerous lumps in their breast was some doubt about their femininity.

Psychologists have said for years that they have observed, in our male-oriented society, the deep desire so many parents have for a son. Some parents want a boy so badly that when a girl is born she is given a boy's name, and she gets the message and works to fill a boy's role in the family. We are all aware of the truth and also the unfairness of this. But I am coming to see that trying to make women see their own uniqueness and power and strength is really stepping into a buzz saw because women just think that Jackie and I are trying to send them back into being male-dominated.

This is so far from the truth. A male-dominated society is a sick society, just as a female-dominated society is a sick society. Our personal experience is that when I become responsible and Jackie can be receptive to that, then we both come into our full power as whole adults, and there is no need for competition. We are complete together—and we are complete separate. We are whole. I am finally truly receptive to Jackie because I am responsible. And Jackie is truly receptive to my responsibility and able to be freed to be responsible for her womanness.

All creativity from both male and female comes from their natures. A whole man is a wondrously creative being. A whole woman is a wondrously creative being. We feed each other, and we both grow with no need for domination. It is my feeling that we have to at least begin this process before we can begin to be "clear." We need to begin to understand our own natures and why we are here and what this world is all about before we can be very clear about anything. And the lack of purpose and clarity and feeling that we are experiencing in our world is, I think, a collective neurosis, which is the outcome of irresponsibility and unreceptivity that has left a majority of us confused and frightened.

My friend Jefferson Campbell from Polarity Institute on Orcas Island in Washington feels that this blurring and shifting of roles is a direct result of war. He feels that war has made babies of men. I would like to see a psychological study done about this because my gut tells me that Jeff is right. Jackie thought this sounded right, too. After the terror of war, what man wants to risk and assume responsibility? They just want to come home and be taken care of. And, of course, the women have been placed in the position of being so strongly responsible while their men were away that they are more than happy to see that they don't have to give up that role and play a big part in encouraging the men to be the babies they want to be. If this has been going on for generations, look at what this might be saying to us.

It's my belief that an irresponsible man can't really love a woman. And an unreceptive woman can't love a man. I think that this is a strong factor in the high divorce rate and the high incidence of drug and alcohol abuse in Western society today. Our families are breaking apart, and I don't see the answer to this in many other theories or philosophies that I have been exposed to.

Jackie feels strongly that women's lib will fail unless men are liberated also. She would rather see a "human liberation" movement based upon seeing the power of our oneness. I see this somewhat differently. I don't think we need any liberation movement because no one has us imprisoned. That's a myth. It's believing the myths in our lives that gives those myths power over us.

One piece of clarity I think almost every human being has to face about themselves is their anger. Most of us have a deep, crucial anger; anger at ourselves, at others, and at life in general. The human animal is, by and large, an angry human animal. A lot of people get very angry at me when I say this!

One of Jackie's favorite "gurus," is Doctor Horst Esslinger. He's a psychiatrist in Germany. He told her, "Jackie! You are such an angry woman." As Jackie tells it, she recognized instantly that she was angry at Horst for saying this to her. What made her the angriest is that Horst said it to her many times. But then he would laugh, and give her a hug and tell her how much he enjoyed angry women. Dr. Esslinger also told Jackie what an angry man he is. From this experience, over and over again, my wife came to accept her anger and lose her fear of this anger.

I tend to flee other's anger and deny my own anger. My upbringing gave me a terror of anger. We are also taught to take the deep, physical emotion of anger and either smother it or intellectualize it or justify it, but never express it unless it is absolutely, positively justified in the eyes of everyone, and then only when the other guy is smaller than we are! We are then in the position of either denying we are angry or looking for someone to hang our anger on where it will look good to us and to others.

Many psychiatrists believe that depression is caused by frozen rage. My friend, Walther H. Lechler, the noted German psychiatrist, believes that most of us have a deep, crucial anger from birth, because in the womb before birth we experienced instant gratification of our needs. We were safe and warm and took food from our mother's bodies even if it destroyed our mother's bones. Then we came through the birth canal into a world that wasn't that safe and warm and instantly gratifying, and this made us angry and generally fearful from the start.

When we were little kids and we got angry at our folks we soon learned that it wasn't safe to show that anger. So we stuffed it or we socked our little brother. We learned all sorts of inappropriate ways of dealing with anger. Most of us figured the safest way was to deny it. But my experience is that anger will not be denied, and it will come out in all sorts of goofy ways, the most common of which is projecting our anger and hanging it on others. And most of us, when we're able to be honest about it, see ourselves getting angry as hell over very small things. When we've taken the route of justifying our anger we have to be always on the lookout for something to get mad about, and this causes us a lot of pain, not to mention the pain we cause other folks.

Jackie and I were doing a seminar in Dallas, Texas, and a woman in the audience admitted that she was an angry woman. Jackie had the woman come up to the front of the audience. The woman then plaintively said, "I know I'm an angry woman. I even see it when I drive a car. I get so angry at other drivers. But what can I do?" Jackie told the audience to meet "a warm-hearted broad." Jackie learned from Horst Esslinger that when she openly admits to herself that she is an angry woman, she is then able to be the warmhearted woman she basically is. Jackie says openly now, "I am an angry woman. I am an ANGRY woman." Embracing her angry nature made it less necessary for Jackie to stuff her anger or justify her anger. When we do this we no longer need to deny our anger or be angry at someone or something. We're just angry and that's okay. It's just a feeling, like sad or glad, and doesn't have to be destructive to ourselves or to those around us.

Who are the people, by and large, who aren't drinking regularly? Alcoholics! When a drunk admits he's an alcoholic, he stops drinking—one day at a time. A drunk who won't admit he's an alcoholic will keep on drinking. The same principle applies to anger. Angry people who admit their anger can then stop being angry—one day at a time. An angry person who denies his anger will never stop being angry. It's clear!

On days that I recognize that I'm basically an angry person a funny thing happens. I see myself get into lots of deals that the world would say I'm entitled to be angry about, but the anger isn't there. I don't have to stuff it or justify it; it just isn't there. What I used to feel was justifiable wrath, just ain't anymore. I deal firmly with a problem and that's the end of it, and no one sees my temper tantrums on that day.

There are days when I'm not aware of my angry nature and I find, to my horror, that I'm mad at the driver in the car in front of me or I've wanted to beat my horse or I've done something negative to Jackie and she's gotten upset, and then I've been mad and gone out to my workshop and ignored her the whole evening, telling myself that it's not my fault that people drive like maniacs or my horse is cantankerous or my wife doesn't love me as I love her. Just beautiful! I've ruined days on end for myself that way because it isn't nice to be an angry man. Who? Me? Angry?

I was angry before I was a year and a half old. My mother got burned in a fire and went off and left me for three years to have skin-graft operations. I was very angry about that! My wife says she was angry from birth. She claims she came from her mother's womb, spit in her mother's eye and said, "I can do it myself, Mother." These are basic, elemental angers. And most of the anger we display as adults are our ways of trying to justify those basic, elemental angers.

When we live lives in denial of our basic, elemental anger we then live hooked on our own adrenalin most of the time. I believe that's how I had the youngest heart attack in my crowd. Denied anger causes that old adrenalin to constantly pump through our bodies. An angry person, in order to live in this world, is forced to either fight, flee, withdraw, or control. That's an awful, exhausting way to live and the result of that kind of life is disease.

When our major defense against elemental anger is fight, we are constantly looking for someone or some situation to be angry about. It doesn't matter who or why. When our defense is fleeing, we actually physically run from situations. When our defense is withdrawal, we use our intellect to fantasize or we ignore what is going on around us and become passive, withdrawn people. When our major defense is control, we use enormous amounts of energy manipulating ourselves and those around us in order to make the world be the way we want it. I see myself using any one of these defenses—sometimes all of them—in any given day of my life.

All of these defenses are neurotic and all of them are powerful. Neurotic people are not weak people. They are fantastically powerful people. It takes enormous energy to be neurotic. When my wife went through her treatment in Germany the thing that struck her the most was the enormous energy that she observed in herself and everyone there. Neurotics use up their energy in their neurotic focus on resentment, anger, bitterness, envy, and jealousy so they come to the end of their day drained of energy. In the years since Jackie returned from Germany she can't believe all of the energy she has left each day now. The same goes for me. As I've put down more and more neurotic defenses I've watched my energy increase. I have easily twice the energy at age fifty-four than I had in my thirties, and I didn't have a heart attack, heart surgery, or a pacemaker then!

It takes energy to control any of our emotions. But I have observed that the quantity and quality of energy it takes to deny or suppress anger is overwhelmingly greater than that needed to control any other emotion. When we can honestly look and see our basic, elemental anger and embrace it as a part of ourselves, we don't become that anger. It is in denying our anger that we become that anger. Embracing anger is like embracing alcoholism, it releases the spirit so that the anger can be removed. We can learn to laugh at our angry side and deal with it in realistic ways. We don't have to do anything with it, we just have to accept it. When we accept ourselves as we are—then we can change.

I am a very angry person. But because I recognize that anger, I spend 80 or 90 percent of my days without any anger. We can get a tremendously high percentage of freedom from that behavior by the simple expedient of recognizing it.

An alcoholic I knew once told me, "What holds the people in churches together is that they assume they have the virtues. In Alcoholics Anonymous, what holds us together is that we assume the complete absence of the virtues."

One of my fondest memories is a woman who told me many years ago, "Jess, I read your first book when I was a patient in a state mental hospital. I saw your arrogance and was so touched by it, because it made me see that if such an arrogant person as you can make it in society, so can I." Immediately this woman and I had a great bond between us because we were both honestly recognizing that we were each lacking the same virtue; we were arrogant rather than humble.

If you want to be in fellowship with your brothers and sisters in this world, assume the absence of the virtues. If you want to alienate yourself from your brothers and from your sisters in this world, assume that you have the virtues. If you want to be beau tiful, just be yourself instead of that phony act you want to put on anytime you're frightened. You have to be clear within first and then without.

My wife and I believe in the denial of virtues so much that we shudder when someone in an audience stands and asks us if we're Christian. Our experience with so many self-proclaimed, "born again" Christians is that they assume the virtues in a most exclusive way, and we don't believe in that. To us truly "born again" people are so aware of their absence of virtue that they embrace the whole world and all religions, they embrace all of mankind. They know they are one with all of mankind. A Pope John practices love not virtue, and that is unifying not devisive.

In order to become properly one with our mate and with our children and eventually with the whole world, we must first see clearly what responsibility and receptivity is. Then from that first awareness we must begin to become clear, open human beings. This is difficult because our whole lives before this have not been clear. We have been fuzzy thinking, confused, closed human beings in many key areas of our lives. A man can be the most responsible major executive of the largest corporation in the world and still be an irresponsible baby when it comes to close, warm, intimate human relationships. The kind of responsibility that runs a big business is not what I'm talking about. That kind of responsibility is something we *do*, not something we *are*. The same thing applies to women. It's intimate relationships that give us quality and longevity in our lives, not our work. We have to get rid of the idea that wealth and business success means anything when it comes to saving our own lives and our dying family structures.

Words! Words are so limited when it comes to life. Read between the lines. Try to get the feeling from what I'm saying to you. So often we're struck by the difficulty of getting this down into words, and that's because we're not talking knowledge of the intellect but of the heart. I think that clearness comes from the heart not from the mind. And it's essential that we find the teachers that are ours. There are many people saying the same thing that I'm saying, but their words are different. It's my experience that a teacher who's right for us has a heart that we know and understand right away. It's a feeling we get when we read our teacher's words. Their words leap up from a page like a beautiful, light, rose petal. Our teacher's words are always clear to us. We recognize the truth in a calm and lovely way.

The truth clearly stated is far less frightening than the truth surmised. So many of us live half-truths out of shame or a sense of protecting ourselves or others. But everyone always knows what's going on, only not in its entirety and not crystal clear. When we deal in half-truths we leave our family and our friends to assume the whole truth. When we have to assume the whole truth we think it must be horrifying. There is nothing that gives more freedom than the whole truth. When a whole truth is known everything is clear and everyone can then deal straight with no hidden fears or devious motives.

My wife has always believed that true freedom comes only when we see that there's nothing left to lose. The false pride of an alcoholic is so obvious when they feel ashamed to have anyone know that they have joined Alcoholics Anonymous. A week earlier they were falling off of bar stools and vomiting on their friends' shoes, but they weren't aware of that! They thought they were invisible then. We all laugh at that example and see how foolish the thinking is, but we do the same things to ourselves over and over again. For some of us it is the compulsion for food. For others it's cigarettes. For others it's compulsive spending of money. For others sex is their compulsion. Whenever we have a compulsion we are slaves. And when we are a slave to a habit we're hurting ourselves and others. But most of us are incapable of seeing ourselves any more realistically than an alcoholic is. We lie to ourselves and others about what we are doing, and our families and friends join us in this conspiracy. But there is a great peace for us when we surrender. When we know that we don't have answers we know that we need help and ask for it. The most discouraging time of all is when we think we have answers. That's the war of the will. And it's a war we all lose.

I used to wonder what surrender was. I used to puzzle about it with a lot of friends. Now I see that surrender is truth. Just that. Nothing else. The truth of us, stated and lived. That's what being clear is, and it takes courage, but the rewards are so sweet. Anyone can forgive truth. It's half-truths we find hard to forgive. And lack of clarity we find hard to understand.

In one of my previous books I said that I have a Ph.D. in psychology but that I'm really a social philosopher. Jackie sees me somewhat differently. She told me recently that the way she has seen me since she was seventeen years old, is as a contemplative. I went and looked up contemplative. It's a person who wonders how people and things are related to each other and how all that relates to God. I saw that was the issue that preoccupies me a good share of the time every day, "How does this relate to that and how does it all relate to God?"

I told Jackie that I had always seen her as a contemplative, too. Jackie said, "See—I knew that you should have been a monk and that I should have been a nun. But then I would have had to find a way to be the nun that took care of washing clothes for the monks and preparing their food so that I could be near you." I think that my kids were always convinced that I was more a monk than a father. My son Mike is always asking me, "What's up, Dad?" My standard answer always is, "Nothing. I'm just thinking." And I can tell this frustrates him, but it's the truth.

Neither Jackie nor I consider ourselves religious people, but our daily journey has always been a rather solitary quest for a God of our own understanding.

For some reason now we both see that the thinking is slowly giving way to action, a desire now to be what we are. There's a beautiful simplicity in that if we can bring it off. When I've observed people who have finally realized that they are at home in their world and that they are one with everything in the whole world, then their little home or farm or apartment becomes the whole world. Then each person who comes into their lives is every person in the whole world, and the simple things of life become very, very important. Then anger and desire and virtue and attainment fall away and life becomes the simple living of it. This is my clarity. This is the clarity that Jackie and I share. This is the clarity that we are striving for in our own lives.

Chapter Ten

YOU CAN'T HAVE ANY BETTER LIFE
THAN YOU HAVE A GOD

A husband and wife called me from Oregon awhile back. They wanted to know if I knew of some town where there were honest and open people they could open their hearts to. They said they had moved from the East Coast to the West Coast searching for this, and were now moving again, this time to Eugene, Oregon.

I told them I had good news and bad news. The good news was that there were people like this in Eugene, Oregon. The bad news was they were carrying their problem with them. The husband was thirty-nine and went on at great lengths about the miserable life he had had.

I was talking to him about surrender, and I finally asked him what kind of God he had. His voice brightened and came alive. I could see he was really prepared to talk on this subject. He said, "I'm an agnostic." I said, "Did it ever occur to you that that's what your problem is?"

He was shocked. No one had ever raised the possibility with him that maybe his miseries came because of the understanding of God that he had.

That phone call was very helpful to me because it was such a beautiful demonstration of how we hold on to our concept of God and are eager to debate the subject at length with anyone who will listen. It doesn't occur to us that our concept of God has more consequences in our life than any other belief we have. We don't see the connection between our misery and some limited conception of God that we have. We each have a God of our understanding, and often that's the problem. If we have a God that does nothing for us, that's what we get—nothing. If we have a God who does nothing but punish us for wrong-doing, that's what we get. If we see a God with all power and nothing but good for us, that's what we get.

Even more crucially, most people don't seem to understand that they can change their concept of God from one that doesn't produce good results in their lives to one that does. People think they're stuck with their God as they understand him which includes the belief that there is no God. That's a form of belief in God because no-God is their God.

It took me a long time and a lot of suffering to learn this. I see now that my whole life has been my search for my God.

I was raised in the little town of Bricelyn, Minnesota. I went to a little, tiny Baptist Church. We had a great big Norwegian Lutheran Church and we had this little, bitty Baptist Church with perhaps thirty or forty families. A very, very small church. That church was a Northern Baptist Church.

You know, as a youngster you've heard about elephants but you've never seen one. But people talk so respectfully of them, you just imagine there must be elephants. Well, I grew up as a young boy fearing two things and thinking there must be some ferocious problem with them. I feared Catholics and Southern Baptists. I had never seen a Catholic or a Southern Baptist, but I feared them.

In our Northern Baptist Churches, the congregations don't respond very much to what the minister says. They are so silent you could hear a pin drop at any time. I think if Christ walked into the church, there wouldn't be a ripple of noise go through that church. You could still hear the pin drop.

I've never been to a Southern Baptist Church, but I've seen some movies and other things. I've heard tell that it isn't quite that quiet in a Southern Baptist Church, and I think that's wonderful.

As I said, we also had this Norwegian Church in town. One time I asked Pastor Jorgenson why they had such a queer burial practice for those Norwegians. I said, "Why is that?" He said, "What do you mean?" I said, "Why do you bury those Norwegians with their heads sticking out of the ground?" He said,

"Oh, that's cheaper than a tombstone and it lasts twice as long." Isn't that awful? But can't you just see Lars and Olie and Muns with their heads sticking out?

We had so many Olies in our little town, and this is really true, that they had front names to distinguish the different Olies. There was Beet Olie because he worked for the sugar beet company. There was Hub Olie, who owned the Hub Clothing Store. And we had Skunk Olie. I don't know what he did. I never got next to someone old enough to know because we moved away when I was fifteen.

I'm in Phoenix now some in the wintertime. Jackie and I live in a little 20-foot travel trailer down in a trailer park in Phoenix. Some of the old-timers from Bricelyn live down there, and they called me recently when they found out I was there. So I'm anxious to go to them and hear some of the stories they have to tell about my father and some of the good old days.

In fact, one of the old guys from Bricelyn, Merle Shirk called and told me an interesting story about my grandfather. My grandfather was the deacon of the Baptist Church. Young Merle wanted to go to the cattle congress in Chicago. It cost about thirty dollars to go down there away back in the 1920s. Merle's dad, Jeff, was well off and could afford the thirty dollars, but he needed someone to take him. They found out that my grandfather was taking some livestock to Chicago, and Muns Munson, a deacon or an elder in the Bricelyn Lutheran Church was also taking some livestock down. There was even a third man going down who was a deacon in the Lutheran Church out in the country where they still had their services in Norwegian.

So Merle was going to Chicago with these three deacons. They got down to Chicago and sat around eating dinner the first night. Old Muns Munson said, "Well, uh-h, I suppose, uh-h, we maybe should, uh-h go to that show." One of the other deacons said, "Yeah." Merle didn't know what they were talking about, but they went to this show where as near as Merle could figure out it said "burly que." So they were in this show, and pretty soon Merle found out what this show was about.

They were sitting there and at one of the high points of the show just two rows in front of them, these two guys stood up and one said to the other, "Gerhart, ain't this something!" It was Gerhart Nelson, who was deacon of the church in Frost, six miles from Bricelyn, and another deacon from another church in the town. So here, three hundred miles from home, were five deacons of the church sitting together at this burlesque house with this young kid.

Merle said, "They all swore me to silence, but they're all dead now so I can tell you the story." He was really good at imitating the accents of these guys, so it gave the story an extra charm.

The ideas in this chapter are what I talked about in January of 1981 when I was asked to speak at Houston Baptist University. I told the people at Houston Baptist that I was happy to have the chance to talk to them about the ideas in this chapter which I hadn't seen clearly enough to get down in the first draft of the book so this talk to them would give me the opportunity to work out my ideas. I told them that if I had been asked to speak to the Texas Optometry Association, I would say exactly the same thing I was saying to Houston Baptist. I wasn't speaking about God just because I was trying to please them. I spoke on God because I saw how important that understanding is in my life.

When I say, "I can't have any better life than I have a God," I speak of God as a person and a psychologist, rather than as a theologian. And why I'm speaking of this topic is not to do anything for any of you. My job is to sing my song. I'm a person who's in search of myself and in search of my being, and I'm trying to get rid of all the things that are not my being. One of the things that is not my being and one of the things I've found is a grave obstacle to my path is to try to do something for someone else or do something to someone else. So what you will hear from me is as clear and as honest a statement as I can possibly make about me, for me, without any regard to you and where you stand.

It is like why does a bird sing. A nightingale does not sing for any reason but that he is a nightingale and that he is simply singing his song. What you will hear from me is my song. I will be speaking as honestly as I can on a subject that, in my experience, is absolutely the hardest subject there is to talk about honestly, which is God. There is no subject, including the subject of sex, where more lying is done than about a person's views and feelings about God.

One of the women who came up to me at Houston and talked to me before my speech was talking about some of the difficulties that she had in her life and I was speaking of some of the compulsions in my life. She was saying, "I didn't realize, and I wasn't honest enough to admit that I had these things earlier." She and I both saw clearly that not only were we not honest enough to admit that we had these things earlier, we didn't even know we had them or that they were problems to us. We were that blind, that asleep. So there has been a great deal of both blindness and dishonesty in my life about the subject of God.

Talking about God is such an emotion-laden subject that I immediately want to please everybody and I want to assure everybody that I'm on the side of the angels and I'm very correct in all things and I'm very upstanding and what have you.

When I went in the Air Force at the age of seventeen, I carried three or four books with me. If I had paid attention to those books and what they told me about my being, it would have been a great career guide for the rest of my life. It showed me where I belonged. Those books were Sigmund Freud's giant book of the *Interpretation of Dreams*, Emerson's *Essays*, and Munsterberg's *The Eternal Life*. Those books are very close to a reflection of my deepest interests in life. Where I got in trouble was I took a big detour from those interests in my desire to make a lot of money and impress a lot of people. So when I got out of college I decided I wanted to be an advertising man and make $75,000 a year and buy a huge house so the people I loved would be impressed by me and, I see now, so they would be frightened by me. I was trying to scare away the people I loved. That was a big detour.

I found later when I got into psychology why I was uncomfortable with Freud's *Interpretation of Dreams*. He had a lot of beautiful explanations of dreams and behavior. It sounded so pat and so convincing. But when I got into psychology, I found that psychology isn't just neat explanations of behavior. Explanation does not mean anything unless the explanation leads to the ability to control or predict behavior.

I had been an advertising man for fifteen years before I took my Ph.D. I had been a husband and a father for a good many years. All advertising men are students of methods of controlling and predicting behavior. Advertising men, football coaches, businessmen; we're all people who have to predict and control behavior. Bum Phillips, former coach of the Houston Oilers, happens to be an exceptional predictor and controller of behavior of a football squad, and unfortunately his old boss at the Oilers didn't seem to recognize his great genius, so poor old Houston is now without that great man.

What I saw was that psychology was prediction and control. And I saw that Skinner's theories on behavior modification and shaping worked beautifully on rats and pigeons. But I couldn't find any evidence that any of the theories I learned about worked very well for people. They didn't even work well in controlling my own behavior.

I could make myself study by giving myself fifty minutes of studying for a ten minute break for an ice cream cone. So I could do some control of my own behavior in some very limited ways but not in anything that was to me very significant.

There are two great debunkers of psychotherapy, Thomas Szasz in America and H. J. Eysenck in England. Both argue that the research on psychotherapy shows it to be almost completely ineffective. I couldn't find a lot of evidence against their ideas.

As a teacher, I found I couldn't control my students' behavior to any great degree. I was trying to teach my students to make an effective speech. My students made ten speeches, five six-minute speeches and five two- or three-minute speeches. While I could see they got somewhat better at making speeches, I couldn't see that I was controlling their behavior.

One of the interesting pieces of research I saw on teaching was a great demonstrator of how much control of the teacher comes from the students. Using Skinnerian psychology, the students in a class shaped the teacher's behavior so he ended up standing at the right corner of the stage. The way they did it was anytime he moved to his left the students would frown, stir around, and cough. The minute he moved to his right, they would start paying attention to him by nodding and smiling. Pretty soon they would have him over in the corner because that was where he was being rewarded from. When he was in that corner they were all fascinated and listening. Different groups of students in different psychology classes have done experiments like that on their teachers and found it works beautifully.

It's a beautiful demonstration of the reciprocal, back-and-forth control that operates in teaching and in my experience in therapy. The therapist is shaping to some degree the client, but the client is also shaping the therapist. It's a lot like a basketball game. There are certain lines on the floor and you stay within those lines and you obey certain rules that the referee reinforces. The more I studied psychology and its applications, the less impressed I was with the results it could produce. I was in psychology for a very different reason than my fellow graduate students. They were looking for a career, I was looking for a way to save my own life because I knew I was in deep trouble.

When I was thirty-five I had had a heart attack. I had seen that my whole life was crazy. I had spent my whole life trying to impress other people so, as I lay on that hospital bed waiting for my wife to come down, I had this clear knowledge that I had poured my life down a rat hole. I said to myself, "I'm never again going to do anything I don't believe in."

I set out at the age of thirty-five to find out what I believed in. And that was a very difficult search because I had never told the truth to myself. I had lied to myself so much that I didn't know what I believed in. So I was a desperate man in search of myself.

After I got my Ph.D. in psychology and taught at the University of Minnesota for a few years I moved to Bozeman, Montana. There I ran into a man named Vince. He proceeded to teach me one of the most important things I had ever learned.

He was an alcoholic. He came off skid row when he was forty-five. He had been sober through Alcoholics Anonymous for five years when he realized he was still bitter and dissatisfied and his life was misery. All he was, was sober. "I'm sober, ain't I?"

After five years of that, he said to his founding fathers, the guys who taught him, "There must be a better way of life. Can you guys tell me what you've got that makes you smile?" And they said, "Vince, you cannot have good, long-term, happy sobriety unless you get the spiritual part of the program."

This was the idea that I was so struck by. I saw that in Alcoholics Anonymous there was a group of people everyone had given up on. The doctors had given up on them, the ministers had given up on them. Nothing is more unrewarding for a minister than to be counseling an alcoholic who gets drunk every day. In the morning they express every hope of reform and that evening they're dead drunk. Very few ministers can continue to counsel that person after about the tenth time that happens.

And the doctors gave up on them—wouldn't talk to them anymore. They broke the doctors' hearts, they broke the ministers' hearts, they broke their wives' and their families' hearts, they even broke their own mothers' hearts. So everybody had given up on the alcoholics. But those alcoholics found in AA a program that could restore them to sobriety.

Here were a million people, the toughest cases, and they were all sober and most of them had found a new, happy way of life. As an experimental psychologist, I was struck by this gigantic experiment with one million subjects. Here were a million people seized by the most powerful compulsion we find in society today. And here was a system that could stop it. I looked at that and asked myself, "What is it? What makes it work?" I started looking at that system and studying it as an experimental psychologist. I came to see the heart of that system is a deep surrender to God—as each person understands him, a higher power, some power outside yourself. That's the crucial part of the system, and without that surrender the system can't get a person sober on a long-term basis, and especially it won't work to give them the happiness and contentment they would like to find in life.

Out of that study of AA, I came up with the idea for what I called "Mutual Need Therapy," which was a therapy based on mutual loving relationships, a mutual deep honest sharing of problems, and a belief in God as a person understands him. This is the process I described in my third book; *I Ain't Well—But I Sure Am Better—Mutual Need Therapy*.

At the time I was working out those ideas, I presented a paper on my observations on AA to the Montana Psychological Association. Some of them were so horrified at seeing the word God in there that they turned my paper over and refused to read further. A few argued with me vehemently. "What are you? Are you a psychologist? This reads like a religious tract," was the way one woman responded.

As a young person, my religious experience was a very unusual one because most people who have had difficulty with religion are full of stories about people presenting religion negatively in their lives. My story is the exact opposite of that. I had nothing but exceptionally loving people in that little Baptist Church. They loved me and were exceptionally kind to me, and I haven't had but two or three even mildly negative encounters with religion throughout my whole religious experience. The limited and negative understanding of God that I had in those early years, I developed completely on my own. I did it without the help of the negative experiences that most people I talk to cite. They say, "I have trouble with God because my grandmother punished me in church," or "I was forced to go to church," or "I was taught a God of fear and anger."

I had none of those experiences. I went to Sunday school because I enjoyed being there. I found there people who really loved me, and I found good things there for me.

Even in those days I did see another aspect of myself I was to see more of later. They kept a chart in my little Sunday school, and you got a star in each one of your little squares for coming. I was very concerned that I not have any squares without stars in. So that compulsion of mine to be concerned with appearances that has been such a problem had already showed itself when I was eight and nine and ten years old. I took pride in the fact that I didn't miss Sunday school like Mark Hunt and Dennis Shirk and Mavis Dahl. They would miss class and I wouldn't. Now that is not a real good reason to have been there. But I was also there for some very good reasons.

I saw another interesting thing. My dad would take my mother and myself to church, and then he would go down to the local tavern and spend the morning with his buddies. This was back in the 1930s when times were really tough and there was so little cash money. Old Reverend Whitby was preaching in an old suit that was frayed at the sleeves. My father saw that it was not good for a man of God to be preaching in a frayed suit so he took up a collection down at the tavern of a buck a head to buy the minister a new suit of clothes. It wasn't the front-row sitters in the church. I could see that many of them felt, "Of course Reverend Whitby shouldn't have a new suit, he isn't working. Our hard-earned money that we donate to the church should go to the important things, like heat and light." So that situation always struck me as odd.

When I was twelve years old, my friends in Sunday school

and I weighed the question of being baptized. I made the decision to be baptized in the very positive way. I was very filled with the feeling of goodness.

They had a baptismal tank under a trap door in the altar in the Baptist Church in Albert Lea, Minnesota, a town thirty miles away. You walk down into the tank where the minister lays you back under the water to be baptized. So we walked down one at a time into the tank and were standing up to our chests in the water and were baptized in the name of Jesus Christ; and we were dressed in white.

I came up out of the water and was standing there watching the next person to be baptized behind me, who was Dorothy Black. She was physically very well endowed. I was looking at her as she came up the steps out of the tank and here she's showing through her white dress. I had just been baptized. I'm right on the altar and here I am full of sinful thoughts. So the other side of my nature was very clear to me again.

We moved away from Bricelyn to Minneapolis when I was fifteen, and Reverend Whitby retired shortly after. I came back to visit at the church when I was nineteen and I remember asking Reverend Patterson who was the new minister, "There must be something more. I'm looking for something more." All I was hearing was words. I wasn't experiencing anything. I see now what it was I was seeking. I was seeking the fullness of the spirit that leads to a fullness of life.

Reverend Patterson was not much older than me. All he could suggest was that I read Butler's *Lives of the Saints*. By then I had already read so many books that I couldn't see where one more would help me.

In Minneapolis, I became a Methodist because they let me play on their basketball team. I was a very clumsy basketball player and consequently I fouled a lot. So I was a real aggravation, but they were charitable enough to let me play on their team so I joined the Methodist Church and went to church and Sunday school regularly.

While I was there, they had an evangelist come on Sunday evening. I had a spiritual awakening. I went down the sawdust trail repenting, making a decision for Christ. I felt really clean and spiritual. I went down to the Marigold Ballroom and told the people down there I had been dancing with regularly on Saturday nights, "Hey, you guys, I'm not going to come back and dance with you anymore. I've got the spirit now."

Guess where I was the next Saturday night? Right back at the Marigold Ballroom holding the girls close. That's how long that spiritual awakening lasted. It obviously did not fall on fertile ground. That spiritual awakening fell on solid rock, and the seed perished very, very quickly.

Now it was a beautiful spiritual awakening. There was nothing wrong with the experience. I don't fault the experience. But it fell on solid rock.

I later became a Unitarian. At the university, even to think about believing in God was ridiculous. Who would dare even ask the question, "Is there a God?" There was this overwhelming conspiracy at the University of Minnesota, "Well, of course there's no God." That's the most difficult thing for a person to handle. It's easier to combat someone who talks against God than somebody who believes the subject isn't worth talking about. That was the feeling I got at the university.

I became a Unitarian, and I was going with the girl I later married. She was Catholic. Her mother was frightened for her daughter. She said to me, "That Unitarian faith, is that Christian?"

The question had never occurred to me, so I started looking at Unitarianism and found it was roughly half Christian and half not. Their magazine, the *Christian Century* magazine was the oldest continuing Christian publication in the country. Half of the Unitarians at that time wanted to take the word "Christian" out of the *Christian Century* title. But the other half wanted to keep it in. I don't know what's happened since then. That was in 1948.

I was nothing for a while, and then I joined the Catholic Church in 1952 and felt a great peace.

Ten years later in 1962 on February 15, I had that heart attack and said I'm never again going to do anything I don't believe in. As I look back, I saw that I did a very interesting thing. Here I had four different religions that I had been a part of, five if you count being nothing as a religion. But I didn't turn to any of them to help me seek what I believed in.

In all of those religions, I had been as faithful a practitioner
as I could be. Typically, whatever one I was in, I was held up as
a good example of somebody in that religion. In my most recent
one, as a Catholic, I would go to daily mass, daily communion,
frequent confession, was friends with the priest, and all those
things. That had been the way it was in all the different church
associations I had.

But because those approaches to God hadn't yielded up to me
what I was seeking, I didn't go there and look. I didn't go
against them. I just said, "I'm never again going to do what I
don't believe in." I started looking in life for what I believed in.
I started looking anywhere and everywhere for ideas that
would help me live better. I even went to a psychiatrist, but he
couldn't do much for me, mostly because I lied to him. I
couldn't tell that rascal what I was really up to, and so he
couldn't do much for me. Isn't that a surprise?

Then in 1966 I found a group of people who would really listen to me. It was like walking into a warm room on a cold day. I
experienced love in a deep sense for the first time from a group
of people. Now, this isn't saying that there wasn't love for me in
the churches I had been in. But my ground was so hard I wasn't
experiencing it. But in that little gathering I found I experienced
love for the first time from a group.

I was talking later to old Vince about this and he said, "Jess,
the problem in the churches and the reason we have so much
trouble with them is that the people in the churches assume that
they have the virtues. To be in the churches you have to assume
that you have the virtues." He said, "We, in our fellowship in Alcoholics Anonymous, we assume the complete absence of the
virtues." (I'm not an alcoholic, but Vince was willing to teach
me anyway.)

If I'm at a gathering and someone wants to find out who of us
is selfish and angry and crooked, and cheats and steals and lies
and overeats and abuses himself in every way known to man,
that's the group I belong in. I belong with the people who have
the complete absence of the virtues.

I've heard it said that a church is not supposed to be a resort
for the well, it's supposed to be a hospital for sinners. I know
that, and I know lots of people in churches say that. But, in my
experience with churches, when I'm talking about my sinning, a

lot of people in churches get awfully uncomfortable and find it very difficult. I've been in Pentecostal and Charismatic groups. If I would speak in the past tense things would be fine. I could say "I was a dope addict and a rummy and all these other things, and now I've had this Christian experience and I'm a beautiful person." No problem. I could say anything about what I did before I had that reborn experience.

But to be talking about the difficulties that I'm having today as a Christian in Christian groups, in my experience, is not very welcome. It was about like Jimmy Carter when he was honest enough to admit he lusted after women. When I say I'm having trouble with arrogance, I'm having trouble with my selfishness, I'm having trouble with the way I isolate myself from my wife and family, people will listen to me but they don't come rushing in and say, "My God, you too, Jess? Boy, I'm doing the same thing. And boy, you should have seen what I did to my own kids last night!" Everyone seems to want to be the good example of how well Christianity has reformed their lives.

So this has been something that for me has been a difficult experience with the formal practice of religion. I've spent a lot of time in the churches, as I've mentioned.

Just before I moved to Bozeman in 1967, I had said to my group that what troubled me was that I didn't have close emotional relationships. Well, the words were no sooner out of my mouth than I realized, that didn't trouble me at all. I had a hundred friends, and everybody would have said that about me. "Oh, Jess has a lot of friends." Yes I did. I had a hundred friends to avoid having any. I would take a friend off the shelf and play basketball with him, then put him back on the shelf and say, "I'll see you in a year." I would take a friend off the shelf and say, "I'll go partridge hunting with you this fall; see you next fall." I had a hundred friends to avoid having any. All of a sudden, I realized I loved not having close emotional relationships. I did not want anybody close enough to me to see what I was like. I was so frightened of what I saw in myself, even though I hadn't looked very deeply. I had just lifted up the covers and peered under them a little bit and put them down very quickly. I was so frightened at what I saw there that I didn't want anybody to know about it. Most of all I didn't want myself to know about it.

I made the decision to change my attitude. "Okay, I'll be

willing to open myself up to friends." I then had to face the horror of finding that the first two people that became friends of mine were both people I looked down on. I asked myself, "What kind of person are you that you cannot have friends unless you can look down on them and feel superior to them." I was horrified at what I saw but I said, "Well, that's me. And that's the best I can do, I ain't much baby—but I'm all I got." Or like Miss Piggy says, "You got to go with what you got." So that's what I did. I went with what I had. And faced what it was.

Then, in Montana, Vince told me about finding out from his teachers that he couldn't have long-term, happy sobriety unless he came to grips with the spiritual part. It was then that he said to me the most amazing thing I'd ever heard. He said, "*You can have whatever understanding of God you want in your life, and you will have the consequences of that understanding of God.*" That was so startling to me because I could not, at that time, conceive of the idea that God could be anything but just one thing. I thought God was God, and that's that. I see now that that's true. The problem was that I was confusing my perception of God with God. The idea that I could change my understanding of God in any way, shape, or form never occurred to me.

The God that I had, even with all the good early experiences I had had, was a God who separated the sheep from the goats and punished the goats and rewarded the sheep. I could see who was going to heaven, and I could sure see who was going to hell.

Now while the climate looked to be a little bit better in heaven, hell was the place where the good company was because all the people I liked were going to hell.

I saw that this God that I understood only had the power to punish or reward in the hereafter. He had no power in affecting my daily life in terms of guiding and directing me in my daily activities like my work, my life with my family, my life with my wife, and my life with myself.

My God had no power in the places I needed power. But Vince said, "You can change all that. You can have a God who has all power, who can do anything. You can have a God who can enter into your life in any way you want, give you constant daily direction, and bring you nothing but good."

"Well," I thought, "there's the God of the Bible and that's it."

But then I started realizing that the Bible is such a complex instrument that I have never met two people who had the same understanding of God out of that Bible. I am particularly struck by the tremendous variation in the different Gods people perceive in the same Bible. There are those who are real students of the Bible who have a vengeful, punishing God, and there are students of the Bible who have a loving, kind God. Then I was able to see, "Yes, there is a tremendous variation in people's understanding of God."

As a psychologist I saw that our understanding of God is filtered through our perceptions of the words of God and our experiences. One big experience affecting our understanding of God is the result of our own parents. If they are harsh and punishing, it's hard to see a God who's all kind and loving. If our parents are kind and loving, it's hard to come up with an understanding of a God who is all hate and vengeance.

So I saw that each of us made a choice as to the kind of God we believed in. As I looked back to the Bible, which because of my upbringing was important to me, I saw that in the Bible there was a basis for the God of love and daily guidance that Vince was talking to me about.

At that time I had been trying to make a deeper surrender to God. From what Vince said I could see why I was having trouble. What sense did it make to surrender my will and my life to the care of God as I had understood him? I could see I was powerless, that my life was unmanageable. It had been suggested to me that only a power greater than myself could restore me to sanity. I saw that many people had derived great benefits from surrendering their wills and their lives to the care of God as they understood him.

I saw that if I made a decision to turn my will and my life over to the care of God as I understood him, that was all there was. Once I have turned my will and my life over to God, there isn't anything left. So we're talking about a complete surrender.

But, as I said, my understanding of God was such that I didn't want to surrender to the God I had. If I surrendered to the God I had, he'd make me a missionary and send me to Africa. Well, I didn't want to be a missionary, and I didn't want to go where it was hot. So that was the consequence of my understanding of

God. How could I surrender to such a God? Why would anyone in his right mind surrender his will and life to such a God?

But, as I started to surrender, what did God do? He sent me to Montana, which is nice and cool, and to be a teacher, which I liked, and later a writer, which I liked even more.

One of the problems that I have in turning my life over to God, that I have fought constantly, is my old idea that the only thing that's God-like is the obvious holy thing. I'm an old public relations man and an advertising man and there's a side to me that's so slick. I'm such a con, I scare myself a lot of times. I know how to talk and act so I come off to you as a lovely, holy person. All I have to do is suddenly parade all my Boy Scout deeds in front of you, suddenly parade my holiness in front of you, use a lot of appropriate language, avoid bad words and say hallelujah a lot of times, and you all think, "Wow, isn't he holy!" But some people would get a sinking feeling in their stomachs, "Ooh, I'm not like that. I'm having a lot of trouble with this guy." Well, you should be having trouble in my case because I'd be conning you.

I had an experience one time that really helped me see this. I heard one of the great Pentecostal ministers on tape, a man I admired and listened to a lot. He was right in the midst of this building oration. I know what oratory is. I know how you build on things, and you build and build to a peak. Then you take that peak and you hold it and then at the end you add a fortissimo and close in a blaze of glory as you walk off the stand because you have accomplished something.

Well, right in the midst of building to this fantastic peak, a baby starts to cry in the audience. You could hear the speaker on the tape having trouble with the baby. Then the baby cried some more and the speaker was having more trouble. Finally Bob says, "Madam, could you please do something about the baby." I thought, "Bob, you blew it! The baby, that's Christ! Christ walked in that room as the baby and said, 'Bob, you're carried away with the sound of your own voice.' And the baby is hollering out, 'Bob, Bob, stop it.' But Bob didn't hear the cry of Christ. Instead he said to the baby, 'You stop it,' instead of, 'Hey Bob, you stop it.'"

What we need to do is when the baby cries, we need to say,

"Whoa, let's hear from the baby," because the mother is sitting there dying and the baby has got something to say, obviously, or it wouldn't be making any noise. You see what I'm saying?

So that's what I see as the danger of the obviously holy things. They're so tempting because they give this great appearance.

The understanding of God I now have is a God who has all power, who means nothing but good in my life. As for my relationship to God, I see it this way: I was born into this world separate and alone. But I don't need to die alone. As I see my life it is for the primary purpose of making my spiritual quest. It is my voyage to God. The way I go to God is to give up my sense of separateness and aloneness, my shell. As I see it, I'll spend my whole life getting that shell off, a piece at a time. I can't completely come to God until my shell is completely gone. As near as I can see, there is only about one in many thousands of us who gets completely rid of his shell. These are the obvious saints such as Pope John, Sister Theresa of Calcutta, Muktananda, and the hidden saints we occasionally stumble on who quietly go through life hurting no one and being hurt by no one.

But the vast majority of us, as I see it, won't cross over that line in our lives; we're simply on a lifelong walk toward God.

With this conception of my relationship to God, pain has a very important function. There is pain each time a piece of my shell is stripped away. But since I need that piece of shell stripped away, that pain is a sign of something very good happening. Hard as that pain is for me, the understanding of the good behind it helps make the pain so much easier to take.

There is a big value to me in my understanding that God has nothing but good for me as opposed to the idea that God wants me to have pain. With that second understanding I don't know if a pain I'm experiencing is sent from God or is a sign I'm out of harmony. With the understanding that God has nothing but good for me, then all pain is a sign I'm out of harmony and need to do something about that pain.

Now please don't take me wrong. I could end up in a concentration camp because some power took over this country and arrested all writers of religious and spiritual matters. But I would not say, "Because I am in this concentration camp, that is pain." It is not. It is good.

184

However, if I'm causing trouble in my home and have my wife or children angry at me, that is not good. That is pain. But being in a concentration camp about to be burned up is not pain, as I'm using the word.

Many people in the spiritual field start talking about the abundant life and all they mean is money and peace and happiness and smiles. I am not talking about that. Most people who have the abundant life will have enough money to pay their bills. Also, they have so few wants that it doesn't take much money to pay the bills anyway.

I'm talking about a God who has all good things in store for me so that when I'm experiencing pain, it is a sign I am off that path. It's just like when you get off the freeway, you start hearing from the gravel along the road, then from the bumps in the ditch, then the telephone poles, fence posts and cliffs and lakes. So pain in life is now a beautiful sign that tells me I'm off the path and need to get back.

My God now guides me in all things. He speaks to me regularly through all the people around me including the crying baby I mentioned earlier. God speaks to me most frequently through my wife.

When Joan of Arc was being cross-examined by the bishop, he was trying to find some way to spare her from being burned at the stake for hearing God's voice. He said, "Don't you think it might be your imagination?" and she said, "Yes, it is my imagination." The bishop was so relieved, he thought, "Thank God, we don't need to burn this girl." But Joan continued, "That's the way God speaks to me, through my imagination."

There's a story about two guys who were sitting at a bar in Alaska. One was an atheist and one was a man of God. The atheist said, "There's no such thing as God." The man of God said, "Why do you feel that?" "Well," the atheist said, "I tried it out one time. I was lost in the snow way up north of here in a terrible blizzard. I said, 'If there's a God up there, help me!'" The man of God said, "Something must have happened, you're here now." "No," he said, "some dumb Eskimo came along and saved me!"

How else can God work but through Eskimos? You and I are all just Eskimos for each other. My wife is my biggest Eskimo.

And boy, do I hate what that Eskimo has to say to me a lot of times, I'll tell you. There's a lot of pain in that.

I see now that I couldn't just sit down a long time ago and come up with an understanding, kind, loving God. I believe I had to give myself up to the love of some of my fellow human beings before I could get a better understanding of love. Many of my attempts to love have been very crude and fumbling, and I often ended up hurting the other as much or more than I loved them. But I did experience love of all kinds from lots of people. So now I can believe in a God who is all love and kindness.

I believe that God has the power and the concern for my well-being that he will literally pick me up and put me where I need to be. But for this to happen I have to be willing to surrender, and I have to be open to the Eskimos who come into my life offering me good things. I see that sometimes I'm like the monkey who reaches into the cage for the banana. His hand is caught by the cage because he won't put down the banana. I see that I sometimes trap myself like that by not being willing to give up something that's really restricting my life.

I see other cases where I have trouble giving up good things God has given me. In my head I know that I never have to give up something good that it isn't replaced by something better. I've even had that experience many times. But it is still hard sometimes to put down the present good thing God has given me so that my hand is empty and prepared to receive the new good thing God has for me.

What I am so grateful for is all that my new understanding of God has given me. I can see now that all my shell, my ego, has to go. I can see that will mean new pain each time a new piece of that shell needs to be removed. Hard as that pain is to bear, I now welcome situations where my pieces of shell can be discovered and through increased awareness by me, given up and removed.

The more shell I get rid of the more cleanly I can love. What counts for me more and more is not loving others but knowing that at my core I am love. Then I can *be* that love without any concern for *doing* loving things or *having* love.

When I'm in my new understanding of God in its clearest way I can simply be love to my wife, to my children, to my family, to my friends, to my community and my horses and to the rest of the world. God lives in me as me. God lives in you as you. So it is all love and all God.

And by my fruits,

. . . by the way I walk
. . . by the way I talk
. . . by the way I act

. . . by my fruits you will know just where I am in my movement toward God—and my surrender to God's grace.

Chapter Eleven

THERE IS A WAY OUT—THERE IS A
LIFE BEFORE DEATH

As I look back over this book and ask myself, "What does it all mean?" the answer I see is: There is a way out—there is a life before death. Before my heart attack I didn't think there was a way out. After my heart attack I hoped there was a way out. Now I see there is a way out.

What I mean by "a way out" is from a story that I've told before but that means so much to me. An old friend of mine at one time was an alcoholic on skid row in Ogden, Utah. He was so far down, so close to death, that he could hardly walk. He was sleeping in an abandoned car. He had saved up some money to buy a warm coat so he could ride a box car over the Sierras to California for the winter.

He spent the money he had saved on wine and woke in jail again. They turned him loose on Sunday morning. He couldn't get any money or wine, so he went to a nearby park and slept.

When he woke up, he saw two guys approaching him who had been on skid row with him. Both of them had been so far down that he had looked at them and thought, "If I ever get as bad as them, I'll do something about it." But he had gotten as bad as them and hadn't been able to do something about it.

The two men walked over to him and sat down on either side of him and offered him a cigarette. They said to him, "Vince, there's a way out." He could see from looking at them that there must be because they both had on clean white shirts and shoes that matched.

These two men told Vince about the program of Alcoholics Anonymous. Vince was forty-five then and just a piece of garbage, one step away from the undertaker. But his pride and obstinacy was finally broken down enough so he could hear. He went to an AA meeting that night where he had to crawl up the steps on his hands and knees to get to the second-floor meeting room. He never touched alcohol again and started down the road to recovery.

That's what I mean by "there is a way out." What I mean by "there is a life before death" came from another story I read in the AA *Grapevine*. A man of sixty-four came into AA. A year later he was so thrilled with what his first year of sobriety had meant to him that he wrote an article with the title, "There is a life before death." Rather than curse the sixty-four wasted years, this man was filled with gratitude for the one year he had been given along with the prospect of more good days to come.

This is where I'm at. A long time ago I didn't understand there was a way out and a life before death. I thought all there was this side of the grave was pain, suffering, and the struggle to learn to cope with life. I thought it wasn't until we crossed over that we could have the victory. I see now that the victory is on this side.

The best way to sum up this book and pull its seemingly divergent threads together is to tell you where I'm at as this book is being finished. My situation today is a beautiful example of what my books have done for me. Four years ago, as I said, Heinze Kappes said, "I walk most safely when I don't know where I go." As that idea has taken root in me and now come to fruition, changes have occurred in me that have become vitally important to me in just the last few weeks. So the book is finished just in time to give me the help and understanding I need to face some crucial days ahead.

The marriage that Jackie and I have had for over thirty years is finally freed from the crucial distractions. We both used to run away from each other and the marriage. Jackie and I are face to face with nothing between us, nothing to hide behind. There's no escaping anymore what we have to do, which is to put down our fears of ourselves and each other.

The writing and speaking and teaching I have done so much of is at a critical juncture, and I don't know which way it is going to go.

I see that Bozeman, which has been so much security for me, may not be our year-around home anymore.

My horses, which were so important to me, I find myself cutting down on. Two of them are loaned to friends now, so only four are in our pasture.

Perhaps the biggest change of all is that the person who always had five plans for early eventuality, me, doesn't have any plans for any eventuality—except one. That plan is the title that ended up on the cover to this book. I don't know where I'm going—but I sure ain't lost.

I know that all I need to do is go ahead a day at a time, putting one foot ahead of the other, and I'll continue to experience in a deeper and deeper way God's abundance for me and my family. I will have God's guidance, a day at a time. That's all the guidance I need or can handle. In an AA tape I heard recently the speaker, Bob E. said it beautifully. Part of what he said was his words, part was quoted from an unidentified source:

> There exists a mystic power that is able to transform your life so thoroughly, so radically, so completely that when the process is completed your own family will hardly recognize you. And in fact you will scarcely be able to recognize yourself. It can lift you out of an invalid's bed and free you to go out into the world to shape your life as you will. It can throw open the prison door and liberate the captive.
>
> This power can do for you that which is probably the most important thing of all in your present state; it can find your true place in life for you and put you in it.
>
> This power is really no less than the primal power of BEING. To discover that power is the divine birthright of all men.
>
> The kingdom of God is within you. Seek first the kingdom and all these things shall be added.
>
> But where is this wonderful power to be contacted? The answer is simple. The power is to be found within you—the last place most people would look for it.
>
> Within us lies a source of energy stronger than elec-

190

tricity, more potent than a high explosive, unlimited, and inexhaustible. All you need is to make conscious contact with it to set it working in your affairs.

I recently had a new understanding of God and how to contact him that was very important to me. It gave me a whole new understanding of life and is of great help to me as I face so much that is unknown.

In *Sex—If I Didn't Laugh, I'd Cry*, I was concerned about the consequences of our steadily eroding family structures. I worried that children reared with less and less touching and love would be increasingly violent and disturbed. This suggested to me a downward spiraling that didn't seem to have any end but destruction.

But recently I've come to a new understanding of that. God isn't up; he's down. All the people I've seen meet God, met him first in their despair, fear, doubt, horror. What I see is that my friends and I went spiraling downward, farther downward into pain and craziness—into chaos. Finally, we went far enough down into the pain and it hurt enough that we cried out for help. That's where we found God. God is down, not up.

People always find God in foxholes when the bullets are flying and the bombs are getting closer. We can see God in the pretty sky at the picnic, but for most of us it isn't an experience that lasts. It isn't an experience that sticks with us the rest of our lives.

As I puzzled this out I was reminded of a book I had read a long time ago. It was a history of the Catholic Church. It told briefly the story of each pope. What was so fascinating to me was that it showed how corruption would move in and take root among the cardinals and the pope. They would be taking graft, giving bribes, and fathering illegitimate children. When the pope died, they would elect a new pope they expected to continue the corruption.

But lo and behold, the new pope would have a spiritual awakening, sweep St. Peter's clean of all the venial cardinals and there would be a period of one hundred to three hundred years of good rule before corruption came sneaking back in for a while, and then the process would be repeated.

I saw that cycle as so hopeful because it showed so clearly that things are never hopeless, no matter how bad they may seem. You can go to any skid row in America today and look at the drunks lying on the sidewalks. What I know, though, is that one out of three or four of those drunks will have a spiritual awakening pretty soon. A year later his life will be cleaned up. He may even have a suit on and be working in a stock market a few blocks from the Bowery. That's what our eyes can't see when we look at a bunch of drunken bums. We think we see reality. But we don't see reality. We see our delusions.

There is a way out; there is a life before death. The fact we don't understand that doesn't mean it isn't happening right in front of our blind eyes.

I have seen so many lives changed that I can understand this now. But it has only happened as I've gotten myself slowed down more.

Most of us can't see because we are in such a frantic pursuit of life. When I first came to Montana fourteen years ago, I was up on the track jogging around. I was on Cooper's Aerobics program marking my points, jogging around in my little shorts with my stopwatch in my hand. Suddenly I realized that there was something about that whole process I didn't like. Then I realized that this was very much like what I was trying to get away from. When I'd had my heart attack I'd quit doing so much competing. I hung up my golf clubs and quit playing poker for money and quit playing chess and bridge. I did it because I didn't want that competitive stuff and all those numbers in my life anymore.

What I saw was that I and most of the other joggers were afraid of death. We were running around saying to ourselves, "If I keep jogging, I'm going to be healthy and I won't have a heart attack." Well, when you do anything with that attitude, you just died. There's no pleasure in doing anything to make something happen. Pleasure comes from process, not from results. That's why you can't manufacture joy. Joy is a by-product; it isn't a thing. All the joy banners hanging in churches can't bring joy. You can't "think joy" and have it. You can't do something physical in order to live longer and get any benefit from it because fearing death is the underlying basis of the exercise, and it's killed your mind and spirit. So, while you can jog and jog and delude yourself that something's happening, it isn't. The person who says, "I want to live. I'm going to live," just died because the flow is gone. Our bodies never benefit from exercise unless the by-product is enjoyment and pleasure.

In an earlier chapter I told you that I gave up sugar. In the stage of growth I'm in right now, I'm clear enough to see that refined sugar, refined carbohydrates are hurting me, so I've stopped using them. But there's an interesting study out now about a bunch of people who the scientists began to study about forty years ago when these people were in college. What they did forty years ago was to first do an emotional study of these college kids and put them into two piles. One pile was emotionally healthy, and the other was not—according to their tests. These people are all in their sixties now, and the results of the study really tell us something. What is so fascinating is that most of the people who tested emotionally unhealthy managed to get really physically sick, and a lot of them died before they reached sixty. The number of emotionally unhealthy people who got really sick or died is tremendously disproportionate compared to those who tested emotionally healthy.

You've all heard about the studies that showed the effects of genetics on your life span. If both of your grandparents lived a long time, chances are you will too. What they found was that this fact didn't help you if you were emotionally unhealthy. And if both of your grandparents died young and you are emotionally healthy, this doesn't affect you either. You'll live a long time.

To the scientists' amazement, cigarette smoking, diet, exercise, genetics, did not seem to affect the people in the study to the degree their basic emotional health did. In the emotionally healthy group of people, the cigarette-smoking people, the people who ate what they wanted, the people who didn't exercise, the people whose grandparents died young were as physically healthy as the emotionally healthy people who didn't smoke or overeat or who exercised regularly and those who had grandparents who lived a long time.

Among the emotionally unhealthy people, those who didn't smoke, or who watched their diet, or who exercised regularly, or who had long-lived grandparents were dying as fast as those who weren't taking care of themselves or didn't have a strong genetic heritage of long life.

Do you see? I can stop using sugars and refined carbohydrates and it isn't going to make much difference if I stay emotionally unhealthy. I can exercise, but if I'm emotionally unhealthy, what good does it do in the long run? The key that makes the difference in how long I live is my emotional health. And I'm not stuck with the emotional health I had when I was twenty years old. The big lesson I've learned from studying the alcoholics who came into AA is that we can change the worst of emotional health to the best of emotional health. That's why most people who come into AA live forever.

We are dying now of all sorts of stress-related diseases because we are stressed people living in terribly stressed chaotic times. Should we throw in the towel and just say, "I give up?" No. This is a terrifically exciting time to be alive. We are on the threshold of a new dimension of life. For the first time in human history we have solved enough of our physical problems and our scientific problems that we can now turn to our spiritual quest. Our journey has just begun. It's no time to give up. It's time to begin.

Jackie's friend Horst Esslinger is a doctor in Germany. He sees this so clearly. He'd tell Jackie over and over again that she would lose weight and keep it off when she changed her way of seeing the world. And not before. What has the way you see the world got to do with diet? Isn't willpower what you need? Isn't it discipline? No. You need something far greater than that. You need to see yourself and your world and your place in the world with a whole new attitude. When you've accomplished that you won't need to diet, you will be just the right weight, and there won't be any effort to it. Our body is crystallized mind and spirit. You can use discipline and lose ten or twenty or a hundred pounds, but you won't keep it off unless your attitudes change and you become emotionally healthy. Emotionally healthy, you won't need to diet because you'll stop eating more than you need to stay healthy. It's just that simple.

A few years ago I couldn't have told you if sugar was good, bad, or indifferent for me. There was such commotion going on inside of me that trying to understand my body's signals was impossible. When we are completely healthy—body, mind and spirit—we don't get signals. There's no need. For most of us, we get signals, but at first we don't even understand them. But as we begin to grow we begin to understand. Slowly we begin to understand more and more subtly.

I don't want to preach the bad effects of sugar because if a person has a sufficiently clear mind, a sufficiently powerful spirit, and a sufficiently healthy body he can eat whatever he wants, and it's no problem to him. You have to understand the interrelationship of these factors.

An emotionally healthy person recognizes and fills his needs. He takes care of himself. What are our needs? They are: Health, love, abundance, and adequate self-expression. My experience is that all are interrelated, and that all are God's will for us. But we seldom truly understand them.

Let's take health. If you are diabetic now or have a bad heart or even cancer, are you unhealthy? No. Even if you are dying right now, you need not have poor health, amazing as it sounds, because health is an attitude. It is attitude that makes you sick and keeps you there.

A person can die in health even though he is suffering excruciating pain. His death is a beautiful thing because he has the attitude of health. A diabetic can be healthy or unhealthy depending upon his attitude. I can be a miserable, unhealthy man with a bad heart or I can be a healthy, happy person who happens to have a bad heart depending on my attitude.

Love. What's love? It too is an attitude. Your attitude makes you lovable. Your attitude gives you love, allows you to take love in and give love out. It doesn't matter if you are old or young, fat or thin, single or married, if you have an attitude of love you are not alone.

Abundance. Is abundance money? No. It is an attitude. Old Ben Franklin said it for money. "If you save only one penny from your wage each year, you are never poor." I know a lot of wealthy people who are poor and a lot of poor people who don't know poverty. It is attitude.

Adequate self-expression. Attitude once again. If you don't express your needs, who is going to guess them? If you won't develop a responsible attitude and be creative, who will ever know you? If you won't clearly make your statement to the world, who knows you're alive? You aren't alive. You're dead already.

Adequate self-expression fascinates me right now. It has so

many facets. It means so many things. Let's just take a look at one facet.

In your day something comes up and you don't express your feeling on the matter. You deny yourself that right for any of a myriad of reasons. You feel it. It lays there. It's in the back of your mind. It affects you two or three days from now. It also affects everyone around you.

When you deny yourself adequate self-expression it really is a tremendous impoverishment of yourself. And it doesn't just affect you. It affects everyone around you.

Jackie began to think of this need in terms of artistic expression. She saw that every human being is born with an artistic nature. We all have been given a gift from God with which to express our soul. And she saw that few of us express this gift.

Think about this for yourselves. A whole book could be written on this basic human need in all of its many facets. Every human being is born creative in one way or another. But as my friend Jeff Campbell of Polarity said so beautifully, "To be creative we have to be willing to be vulnerable." And that is a terrible responsibility.

Being vulnerable means taking risks. Being vulnerable means becoming able to put your business out on the street; becoming willing to show your true nature to everyone.

My wife calls this, "Learning to take." We all want to be givers. It's safe to give. The risk lies in taking from the world. She saw the truth of "taking" one day when she looked at a tree. She suddenly realized that the tree would have nothing to give if it had not first been willing to take the rain. A "taker" to her is an open person; a person who is willing to be taught. A giver sees himself as a teacher. The dichotomy is that true teaching takes place in this world by the people my wife sees as "takers," because only in being open and willing to learn are we able to store up enough to give.

One of my teachers, a truly great teacher, is Ray Hunt. He teaches horsemanship all over the west from Texas to Canada. At breakfast one morning Ray and I were talking about teaching and Ray said, "I don't teach. You can't teach anyone anything. I'm just an ordinary guy doing my thing that I like to do and sharing what I learned. If someone there is ready to learn, they learn it. But I don't teach them. It's up to them, not up to me."

Jackie's concept of "take" and Ray's concept of just being himself are two different ways of saying the same thing. What they are saying and what I am saying when I say, "everyone knows exactly what to do for themselves" is also basic in many religions.

Jackie was telling Ray Hunt about her concept of "take," and Ray said a beautiful thing to her. "Jackie, I see what you're saying. You use the word 'take' to arrange these ideas for *your* mind. Everyone has to find the way to arrange these things in their mind so that *they* can understand it." This is so true. That is why there are so many roads to Rome. Each of us must find our own guru.

An interesting thing happens to people when they finally become willing to learn how to live. They quit dying! I saw this in Montana. I have a lot of friends all over Montana in Alcoholics Anonymous. I'm not an alcoholic myself, but these people let me come to their open meetings because they know how bad I need what they have. There was one guy there who'd been a heavy drinker for over forty years. Mayo Clinic told him that he had only about a year left to live shortly after he sobered up because of all the damage alcohol had done to his body. That was more than twenty years ago. This guy's almost eighty now. There are lots of these old types in AA. The interesting thing is that they don't die.

Seeing these people in AA, who had lousy mental health in their drinking years, made me understand that we can all live longer, more fruitful lives, when we became willing to change our attitudes and become emotionally healthy. If we survive years and years of negativity, if it hasn't killed us yet, there's still time! This is the magnificence of our human body and mind. It has recuperative powers beyond our wildest imaginings. The day we become willing to do something is the day the healing starts. Is it going to be immediate? No. It requires persistence on our part despite all evidence. We have to believe. I don't acknowledge instant miracles. There are a lot of supposed instant miracles. Usually what they are is a surge, a gift from God to put us on the track. But to hold on to that, a person has to be willing to work daily. Now, that is the true miracle: the doing of our work. When we finally come to see that we have the power to heal ourselves if we will devote ourselves to it and not demand it of God, that is the true miracle. We become humble and therefore teachable. Then our doctors and our ministers and all of the others who are there to help us can finally get on with their work.

The acquiring of emotional health is a minute-by-minute, day-by-day, week-by-week, year-by-year learning. There is no easy way. But that learning *is* life. It is the process of life, and that is the part that is so difficult for us.

When that sixty-four-year-old man said, "I have found that there is a life before death," he was saying that he finally stopped acting like a poor, dumb beast and began to live as a responsible human being grateful for his life.

There was a study done about when old people die in relation to their birthday. Do you know that about three times as many old people die in the six months after their birthdays as in the six months before their birthdays? That's an interesting fact and shows us that it isn't so unaccidental when we happen to die. If all we died of was sickness, the figures would be the same. But those figures show that a lot of us can hold on for another six months so that we can reach that next birthday, if we've a mind to. Now I recognize that for many of us there isn't enough to live for. Death is sweeter than life to some old people. That's okay. We all have the right to let death take us when it comes to us and we're ready for it. But a lot of us are hurrying up the process.

It's suicide we're committing. Suicide isn't just the guy that takes a gun and blows his head off. We have to see that choosing to persist in poor emotional health is suicide, too. Alcoholism is suicide. Drug addiction is suicide. Neurosis is suicide. Choosing to live an isolated life is suicide. All of the many ways we use to run from life are suicide. We have to take responsibility for that. A lot of us die from giving up. When we don't see that there is a life before death, we don't see any reason why we should go on.

I don't care what your misery is, there is a way out. For many of us, strange as it sounds, the way out of our misery is to quit trying to find a way out. I've seen crippled people, people with bad hearts, people with cancer, people who were terribly poor find the way out by simply accepting the facts. When you quit running from fear, from pain, from anger and turn with courage and embrace it, you change it. I've seen this happen over and over. When you work with reality, when you embrace it with love, you transform it. Does it go away? Not always. But it doesn't consume you anymore.

When I was a boy I was poor. I couldn't stand having bean sandwiches for lunch when the other kids had lunch meat. I couldn't stand wearing clothes someone gave us because we were poor. I couldn't stand the misery of hearing my dad say, "If I could just get my hands on fifty dollars, I could get through the winter." I couldn't stand having the power company turning off our electricity because the old man couldn't pay the bill. I couldn't stand the way my mom and dad fought with each other when there wasn't any money.

I bent my whole life out of shape and almost died of a heart attack before I was thirty-five trying to be rich. I wasn't an out-and-out thief, but I was always coveting. Even when I had enough money to live better than most I couldn't relax. I had to buy. One day, not too long ago I had to realize that I was a compulsive spender. I'm a spendaholic. When I realized this I suddenly knew that I could never make as much money as I felt I needed because there wasn't that much money in the world. I knew that I would always be poor unless I recognized that I was powerless over spending and was willing to be restored to sanity. That realization was a big relief for me. I stopped running away from my poor childhood. It was a big relief for Jackie, too. She cried, she was so happy for me. I faced my pain, and then it could be dealt with.

I'm fifty-four years old. I learned a new thing about myself through this experience, and I'm able to be more alive today because of it. We are never too old to face ourselves, or too young either. All it takes is the humility to quit fleeing our true nature, a willingness to put down our fear and a willingness to change.

Some people believe that our overwhelming preoccupation from birth is our death. All we vary in is our willingness to recognize that. Look at the way men go crazy in their forties and fifties and get rid of their wives and go out and find a younger woman. Look at how much money women will spend on some preparation to stop wrinkles or color their hair. Or in the extreme, look at the amount of money spent on plastic surgery to lift up anything that is sagging. It isn't just young people who adore youth. Old people adore youth, too, and so they have lost their power, their credibility. If older people believed in the beauty of age, they wouldn't be fighting for respect and a place in this world. How can young people respect anything that has lost its dignity? Human dignity lies in being exactly who and what we are. We recognize that there is no dignity in a ten-year-old girl who's allowed to wear a padded bra and lipstick, yet we refuse to look at the ways in which we deny what we are.

We all see ourselves doing a lot of foolish things in an attempt to prolong youth and to evade or avoid the idea that we're growing older.

Look at the foolishness of not telling birthdays. Anyone can guess a person's age within three or four years either way. So who is anyone fooling except themselves with this coyness? And weight! Most women won't divulge their weight. Yet everyone can tell their weight within a few pounds. It's the same foolish indignity. And we all practice some of it. We must accept ourselves just as we are or there can never be any change. We must quit playing these lying games with ourselves, and I'll tell you why. We must stop because we all know the truth deep inside of ourselves and are diminished as human beings by our lies to ourselves and others.

We need to understand that we are responsible for our days, that we are responsible, by our attitudes, for how we react to everything in our lives. And we have the choice between creating our own heaven or our own hell right here on earth irrespective of what is going on around us. We can have absolute peace and dignity and some joy in our lives in the most miserable of circumstances. Or we can have agony and anger and sorrow in our lives in the best of circumstances, depending on how we choose our attitudes.

As we do our work, and do it in a wider more pervasive fashion, as we start following all of the thousands of clues that our lives provide us with, we can really get hold of the life that is there waiting for us, the life that is being offered to us. Just wake up! Just look around. Just pay attention.

When some of my readers write to me or ask me in seminars, "Jess, tell me what to do," I think of the story of General Patton I told earlier in this book. His officers were always wanting Patton to tell them what to do. It didn't matter that Patton had already told them ten times over again what to do, they didn't want to risk. They didn't want to be responsible. So it was always—"tell me what to do."

Confusion always comes from irresponsibility, from not being willing to risk. We'd rather dig in and die than stick our necks out and take a risk and let ourselves be known. We all act as though "I" had something to hide or something about ourself that is so unacceptable. Some of us have turned this around by now and are living the opposite. Some of us have decided that "I" am acceptable, but the rest of the world isn't. It's the same coin. It makes no difference the reason you give for seeing yourself as separate and alone, it's the basic attitude that's screwing up our lives. Over and over I see all of us get direction that we refuse to listen to.

Always, around us in a given situation, there is counsel available to us. God speaks to us through the people around us. God does not appear personally before us to give us our marching orders. When we quit waiting for what we have decided is divine guidance and start paying attention to reality, we always know what to do. The truth is there in the people around us. God speaks to me to save my own life if I will pay attention. The most often used way that God has to speak to me is through my wife. This is true in every marriage.

God's counsel for our lives is all around us. It's flooding in there. We're getting God's counsel through the people around us, through the situations around us, through our intuition, through our imagination, through meditation where we seek guidance. What more do we want? If God came to us in a golden chariot and said, "This is what I want you to do," we'd begin to doubt the minute he was gone. And furthermore, we'd begin to find reasons not to do it if it involved risk, responsibility, and change. We want things to be different, but we don't like change. We'd rather die the way we are than live a new way.

I know God wants abundance for all of us. The guy that stands in the way of God's abundance for me, is me. If God gives me abundance in money but I manage to spend it faster than I get it, I can prevent myself from having abundance. Right? I see a lot of people who manage to create poverty out of abundance. That isn't much of a trick. That's pretty easy to do. I also see a lot of people being offered abundance who turn it away. A lot of people frustrate abundance out of a false sense of unworthiness. That's irresponsible.

We can live this life before our death in one of two ways. We can be alive or we can be dead already. The choice is ours. And the choice is one of attitudes. My friend Blanche from Odessa, Texas, said a beautiful thing in one of her tapes. She said, "I took on the monumental task of changing the world by changing my thinking."

I have told you my ideas and my experiences here as well as I can. I hope you use them as one of my readers did who wrote me and said, "I have used your ideas to find my own." That's beautiful because I don't write these books to bring you to my way of thinking. I write them so I can state, as clearly and honestly as possible, my own ideas and experiences. Many readers have told me how much it has meant to them to see the growth I've had from one book to the next over the twelve years I've been writing. But there's also change just during the time I'm writing each book, particularly this one. As I do the final revision of this book I'm struck by how differently I think and feel from much of what I've written. Part of me wants to start writing the book all over again. But the wiser part of me says, "Let it go. What's in you now is for a new book down the road aways after you've lived out what's just dawning inside you."

In the last two months there have been some amazing fruits of the central idea in this book that is its title. Another way of saying it is, the proof of the presence of God is finding yourself someplace where you don't expect to be. In so many ways, I'm finding myself where I didn't expect to be.

The biggest example is how I feel inside. I've lost that frightened little-boy feeling that had been with me all my life. In recent years the frightened little-boy feeling would be very dim at times, but it was always there. I can't see a trace of it anymore. I feel at home in the world. For a chronic outsider that is really some feeling.

Franny and Zooey's prayer in J. D. Salinger's book was to see Christ in the fat lady. I see now that we need to go one step farther and see Christ in ourselves. For slim, young attractive people as Franny and Zooey, it was very hard to see Christ in the fat lady. But, ironically, it was even tougher for them to see Christ in themselves, and also, for any of the rest of us to see the same thing.

It has been very hard for me to accept one of the central parts of my character. I thought what would be hard for me to accept would be what I saw as some of my big imperfections. Instead, it is an aspect of myself that is part of my perfection that I have trouble accepting and that I have spent so much time denying and running away from. It wasn't until I had become ready to hear it and experience it and heard it from one of the greatest men of our time, that I could accept it in me.

When I read Albert Einstein's humble admission of his own aloofness (which I quote below), only then was I able to face and own up to that aspect of myself. Einstein was quoted by Sagan in *Boroca's Brain* as saying:

> . . . My passionate interest in social justice and social responsibility has always stood in curious contrast to a marked lack of desire for direct association with men and women. I am a horse for single harness, not cut out for tandem or team work. I have never belonged wholeheartedly to country or State, to my circle of friends or even to my own family. These ties have always been accompanied by a vague aloofness, and the wish to withdraw into myself increases with the years. Such isolation is sometimes bitter, but I do not regret being cut off from the understanding and sympathy of other men. I lose something by it, to be sure, but I am compensated for it in being rendered independent of the customs, opinions and prejudices of others and am not tempted to rest my peace of mind upon such shifting foundations.

When my wife read me that statement of Einstein's, it explained so much to me about me. That aloofness of mind has driven my brother and my kids crazy. So often I'm like quicksilver; squeeze me and I'm gone. Some of this aloofness is gradually leaving me, and there have always been a few people whose company I enjoy tremendously. But there is a sizable strain of aloofness in my nature.

I see now that rather than continue to try to change that aspect of myself, I'll surrender to it and see what God does with me. What a relief that is. I can just give up the struggle to change a part of me that wouldn't change and turn it over to God and let him handle it.

Another big thing that has been different in my life this past two months is the surrender prayer. Each morning, first thing, Jackie and I together read the surrender prayer out loud:

> God, I offer myself to you—to build with me and to do with me as you will. Relieve me of the bondage of self, that I may better do your will. Take away my difficulties, that victory over them may bear witness to those I would help of your power, your love, and your way of life. May I do your will always.

This was an idea we had come close to often; when we heard Bob E.'s tape where he mentioned the fruits of this prayer, Jackie and I decided to start it. For us the results have been amazing.

One fruit is that now I can see that my life is in perfect order. Some of the things I used to think were problems are just circumstances that are smoothly working themselves out.

So more and more deeply I see and experience that God is in me. The kingdom of God is within. God lives in us as us. We were created in the image and likeness of God. Each of us is a unique manifestation of God. So to know ourselves is to know God.

God lives in me as me. God lives in you as you. May the God in me touch the God in you.

I've enjoyed this chance to work out these ideas and to be a part of your life. I salute you with love and respect. May we both go with God through our days.

EPILOGUE

An epilogue is a concluding section that rounds out the design of a literary work. That's ironic because this book all of a sudden needed an epilogue.

Between the final editing of the manuscript of this book and this editing of the galley proofs, I had another big change in my life. I had heart surgery at the Arizona Heart Institute in Phoenix, Arizonia on April 20. I had a checkup there, and they found my two left main arteries were over 90 percent blocked at the top of my heart, but down below these narrowings the arteries were clear and open. The doctors recommended immediate surgery, and I decided that I had no other option. I had three bypasses. This was a problem that existed in my arteries when I had heart surgery fifteen years ago. That was before bypass surgery had been perfected, so it couldn't be fixed then. Over the years, the narrowing of the arteries had increased to the point where recently I started getting heart pain when I exerted myself. So I was very fortunate again to be in the right place at the right time.

I'm in good shape now and once again God has given me good health that, God willing, will carry me many more years. I'm going to use this new lease on life to continue to do my work.

The changes in my life will be reflected in the two books Jackie and I are working on: *Marriage: A Spiritual Affair*, and *The School of Life*, which will be the talks, questions, and answers from the School of Life which was held in Phoenix in January 1981.

I'm grateful for the freedom and good health God has given me. I'm grateful for all of you who were around to help pull out of me the ideas I needed to learn in my own life. The peace I feel now is very deep, and I'm happy to have it. And I don't know where I'm going, but I sure don't feel lost.

My best to all of you.